Tehrangeles

Ben Cuddon

ISBN:1721794549
ISBN-13: 978-1721794546

Chapter 1

"Josh?"

Silence. Josh sat gazing into space.

"Josh. Are you listening to me?"

He continued to stare. His eyes were transfixed on the girl at the bar. He couldn't figure out whether she was the one he'd randomly hooked up with in his freshman year or not…

"Josh?"

Josh shifted in his seat, adjusted his gaze and focused on the frowning, irate face in front of him.

"Sorry. Drifted off. You were saying…" He reached for his drink and took a sheepish swig, stealing one last glance at the girl, deciding she probably wasn't the person he was thinking of. He refocused his gaze in front of him.

"I was saying… I was *saying* you just don't understand where I'm coming from. All the time you keep promising you'll listen to me, but you keep on behaving exactly the same. It's as if nothing changes."

"Right," Josh said, making a genuine effort to engage now. "But the thing is, I don't see… I don't really see…" His sentence trailed off.

"Josh, I'm getting to the point where I just can't be bothered any more, you know? I can't face the nonsense and lies and endless idiocy. I really am going to have to do something serious. Josh? *Josh?*"

Josh's gaze had once again wandered over to the other side of the room. On second thoughts, he now felt certain it *was* the same girl. She'd been out of the light before. But, now her face was clearer, he could see that it definitely was her. My God, he thought. She'd changed. She really had changed.

"Josh!" Natalie's voice came suddenly, like an alarm clock bursting into life, jolting him to attention.

"Sorry," he said, turning to face her properly now. "You were saying?"

The bar was dark and gloomy. The smell of stale ale wafted up from the dark wooden tables and there was a slight stench of urine from the toilets at the end of the corridor. The soft, dark carpets were covered in grubby stains and groups of noisy undergraduates huddled around tables, gossiping about which Final Club had punched them, who would participate in Primal Scream, who would flunk out by their mid-terms. At their table in the far corner, Natalie sighed and looked at Josh, her face a picture of silent despair.

"Look," he said. "I'm sorry. I really am. And the thing is, you've got a point. I need to stop acting like some kind of juvenile idiot. I need to start listening. I'm sorry it's taken me so long to see it."

Natalie stared at him. She felt she might actually be generating light steam from exasperation.

"Have you ever taken a look at yourself? You sit around like some kind of sloth, vegetating and slowly sapping life out of the world without giving anything back. You expect life to deliver itself to you on a plate. You think you're destined for all these wonderful things but the reality is, ultimately, you're still at the same point as ten years ago. I mean, you're really just a *child*." She was so disgusted that she could barely produce the words. Shaking her head in disbelief, she picked up her glass of wine and took a long, therapeutic gulp, staving off the rising tide of fury inside her.

The last few months had been hell. Constant bickering and recriminations. A seemingly endless cycle of fall-outs and make-ups. The problem was the two of them had never really understood each other. Josh had entered into the relationship in a casual jaunty way, Natalie had reluctantly accepted him and then it had grown serious. But he had never been equipped for anything long-term. The longest relationship he'd had was with a German girl he once met at a resort in Florida, and that had only lasted ten days. For some reason, he found staying with one girl for a prolonged period of time an insurmountable challenge. It wasn't because he was a philanderer. It was just that relationships seemed to demand a level of energy and commitment that he couldn't seem to find–at least not at this stage in life.

"I mean, what I don't understand," Natalie continued,

refreshed from her latest gulp of wine and giving up suppressing her anger now, "is how you can adopt a position of such extreme indifference–such nauseating insouciance–when the simple stark truth is that you've put not a single drop of energy into this relationship the entire time we've been together."

"Hang on. I think you're being unfair now."

"You *never* call me."

"I do…"

"You *never* take me out for meals."

"I took you to *Berryline* last week…"

"And the fact that you got me some out-of-date *potpourri* for my birthday…"

"It was ecologically friendly."

"It was from *Freecycle*…"

"That's what I meant by eco–"

The glare from Natalie–like a viper about to lash him with venom–stopped him in his tracks.

They fell back into silence. Josh took a sip of beer. He cast a look across the room, feeling slightly hurt now. On that occasion, he felt he had actually tried. She was always lecturing him about 'taking responsibility'. He'd done something to help the planet, and now she was criticizing him for it.

"And anyway," he said, "it wasn't *Freecycle*… it was *Craigslist* freebies…"

"I don't care!" It stung him like the violent lash of a whip. "I don't care if it was *Freecycle*, or *Craigslist*, or from the trash, or whether you somehow magically regurgitated it out of your stomach. You can't fob people off with recycled gifts Josh."

She sighed and seemed to collapse in her chair, like a snake that has spent its poison. A bee without a sting. She had given all her violence and lashings. They hadn't worked. Now she had no energy left.

"And the other thing," she said, feeling weary now, "is that you haven't remembered our anniversary since… forever."

"Our anniversary?"

"Don't tell me…"

"I didn't think we had an *official*…"

They fell back into silence. Josh felt the moment had come for him to try to salvage the situation. He reached out across the table in a sort of southern Mediterranean shrug and looked at her with long, droopy, sympathetic eyes.

"Look… come on, Nat. I know I've been a crap boyfriend. I know it. But I'll make it up to you. From now on, I'll remember all our anniversaries. I'll meet you any time you like. I'll be really attentive. Forgive me, Nat. Come on, please."

She looked at him with the face of someone who has undergone sleep deprivation for a week.

"I'll call you every evening…"

Silence.

"I'll take you to *JP Licks* whenever you feel like it…"

More silence.

"I'll make you chocolate brownies with salted caramel sauce…"

Natalie looked searchingly at his face, exploring him for signs of honesty, desperately trying to find something to give her hope.

"*Please*…?" Josh said, with all the saccharine schmooziness he could muster, so much so that even he cringed slightly as he said it.

"No." Her voice was emphatic now, the exhaustion giving way to steely-minded conviction. She pushed her glass aside. "I've decided. Enough is enough. I'm sorry, but I just can't go on with this. I need a break. I need a break from this awful, damaging relationship. And that break is coming *now*."

She stood up. "Look, Josh. I'm not interested in your excuses. I'm not interested in hearing you grovel, and apologize, and suck up to me. I'm not even interested in hearing what you're going to get me for my birthday. I'm sorry. I've had to deal with enough of your crap. Today is the end. We're finished."

She pushed her chair back with a piercing screech, like someone scratching their fingernails down a blackboard. Everyone in the bar turned and winced. She stood over him now like a towering giant, bringing forth one final surge of energy to unleash the full power of her wrath upon him.

"I always thought you'd be a friend for life, Josh. But now I'm afraid I'm going to look back and see the last two years as a huge mistake. And as for you? Well, I don't want this to sound harsh, but the simple fact is I'm going to see you as just some prick I once met."

She grabbed her jacket, hurriedly shoved her arms into the sleeves then pushed her chair in behind the table.

"I just hope you wake up Josh. Because you've got a big gaping hole where your heart should be."

Then she stormed out of the bar.

Chapter 2

"She *what*?"

"She dumped me."

"She *dumped* you?"

"Yes, she dumped me."

"Man, that is harsh. That is, like, real harsh."

In Harvard Yard, Josh sat with Louis and Zak under a tree, their backs against the trunk. Students hurried back and forth across the lawns, clutching books under their arms, dashing to lectures. Warm spring sunshine filtered through the trees. Josh stared at the grass, then at the philosophy book next to him. All those sayings of dead white men weren't much good to him now.

"But she couldn't have," Louis said, after a pause. "I mean, she couldn't have just done it out of the blue?"

Josh continued to stare glumly at the grass.

"And anyway, look, Josh… you're the one who was damaged in that relationship. *You're* the one who suffered."

Louis adjusted his cap. He was kitted out in full Harvard regalia–T-shirt, cap, sweat pants. He looked, as his friends liked to say, like an official Harvard mascot. He was secretly proud of the title, except when he got photographed by tourists, an experience he found slightly inconvenient.

Josh raised his eyes from the grass and looked at Louis with his best feeling-sorry-for-himself look.

"I mean, just remember what happened," Louis said, "on your last birthday. What did she make you do?"

"Purse shopping in *Macy's*. For three hours."

"And when you were struggling with your Econ mid-term, did she give you any help?"

"Not really."

"And what about that time you threw up at the Dunster foam party? Did she show *any* inclination to nurture you back to full health?"

"No."

"Exactly. Point made. There is no way–absolutely no way–she

can complain that you've let her down. If anything, I'd say it's the other way round. If anything," he jabbed his finger into Josh's side, "I'd say you've been on the end of prolonged, systematic and far-reaching abuse."

He pulled down his cap, emblazoned with a capital *H*, then leaned back against the tree and settled down, like a dog readying itself for sleep. "I've got a point," he muttered, "haven't I, Zak?"

Zak, silent up until now, turned to face them. His pale, sunken face conveyed a whole lifetime of thought condensed into the body of a twenty-two-year-old. He put down his dog-eared volume of *Chinese Mountain Poetry* and turned to address them.

"It's a complex situation. You've got to assess the full balance of forces. You need to consider the yang and the yin." He took a long drag on his joint. "But, yes, overall I would say you have been completely screwed over."

Louis punched Josh in the side to emphasize his point.

Josh quit plucking blades of grass from the ground and flung them down in a little heap. He looked across the lawn, trying to find alleviation from his despair on the horizon, but found only Widener Library–a reminder of all the reading he hadn't done so far that year. He turned to face the others.

"Look, I hear you. And suppose I *have* been mistreated. I'm not saying it's true. But suppose I have. It doesn't actually change much. The fact is I'm still dumped, I'm still alone, and therefore I'm still, once again, returned to my usual state of desperate, unwanted single man, with what would appear to be not a chance in hell of holding a serious relationship for more than, at last check, ten days."

He plucked another clutch of blades of grass from the lawn, briefly played with them in his hand, then let them fall to the ground.

"Basically, I'm still a loser, is what I'm saying."

"No," Louis said, murmuring in semi-sleep from under his cap. "You're not a loser. Whatever might have happened, you can't let this get to you. Shit happens. You've got to haul yourself up, dust yourself off, and try again. You can't let one sucker punch knock you out. You've got to be stronger than that. Right, Zak?"

Zak took another long drag on his joint and blew a succession of smoke rings into the air. He stroked his wispy blonde beard and readjusted his Indian homespun cotton shirt. He waited until all the smoke rings were released.

"You've got to be philosophical. There are plenty more fish in the sea. Admittedly, we *are* in a small sea here. But nevertheless, it is a sea, you are a fisherman, and you can catch yourself a salmon. If you look hard enough." He looked over at Josh with his eyebrows raised to emphasize the point, then slowly brought his joint back up to his mouth and took another drag.

"OK," Josh said, "so take it I have been mistreated. What next? How do I go about rebuilding my life from this desperate situation?"

"What you do," Louis said, "is put all the crap memories behind you, draw a line under what's happened with Natalie and say: from here on, I am a new man. I will not let anybody stand in my way. In other words, go out into the world and conquer anyone and everyone. Remember, no man ever went to his grave wishing he'd loved one fewer women. Right, Zak?"

"Not exactly the way I would have phrased it, but I think Louis has a point. Be reflective. Be measured. Know who you are and what you want. And yes, as Louis said, quantity is quality. Go and shag the hell out of the female species as if your life depended on it."

There was a pause. Josh plucked another clutch of grass. He played with it in his hand then threw it up and let the blades scatter through the air.

"OK," he said. "So be it. From here on, no messing around. I'm turning over a new leaf. Gone are the days of being a doormat for everyone to wipe their feet on. No more failing to stand up for myself. From now on, I stick up for myself in relationships...no matter what."

Zak looked at him cheerfully, a faint smile on his gaunt face. Even Louis stirred, looking out from underneath his cap.

"Couldn't have said it better myself."

"No matter what," they echoed.

"To the future…"

"To the future," they echoed.

They let out a small cheer that paled across Harvard Yard, like the bell in the memorial tower, and Josh felt some trace of vivacity and energy rekindle inside him.

Chapter 3

Formal lessons began the following week.

That semester, Josh had opted for all the easiest classes he could find. So far, his college career hadn't been a stunning success; solid grades in softer options, such as *Cinema before the Talkies* (many happy hours in Lamont Library watching films) and *East Asian Poetry* (his haiku formation had reached near perfection), had been undermined by results in *Pseudorandomness* and *Early Medieval Latin Literature*, both of which he had failed spectacularly. That wasn't good. He needed his GPA to be respectable. His parents would be furious if, after four years of Harvard tuition, he came out with less than a three.

So this year he was playing it safe. It was back to basics: solid options, minimal coursework, and the chance of failure a remote, inconceivable possibility. Hence enrolling in *Fulfilment 101: Habits for Happiness*. Surely that would be a breeze. I mean, he wasn't exactly a master of being fulfilled himself, but how difficult could that one be? And the one on the art of persuasion. He was immensely persuasive. He would easily get a top grade in that one. Plus one more in art history that consistently had the highest ratio of female to male students. He did feel a bit cynical taking that one. But he had earned his way to college - if he couldn't indulge himself a little bit while here then what was the point?

His first class of the week, *Fulfilment 101*, met in the *Science Center* lecture theater. As Josh entered, students slid into the rows between the seats, the buzz and chatter of expectation filling the room.

Just before 11:00 a.m., the professor appeared. He was bearded, his tweed jacket too small and his bow tie crooked. He fumbled around looking harassed, with a general air of distress. Josh wondered why someone who seemed to be rather unhappy was giving a course on fulfilment.

He shuffled his papers, then looked up and addressed the room.

"So, class. Attention, please. Thank you."

Ripples of chatter faded away as the students settled their attention on the professor. He looked around the hall at the sea of faces.

"You are supposedly the elite," he said, hands on either side of the lectern. "The finest minds in America. You've made it through three years. And now we're about to send you out to make your contributions to the world. We hope they will be great contributions. You are the cream this country has to offer.

"But your toughest challenge still lies ahead of you. You will only be great leaders if you can understand that core concept: fulfilment. If you can master it, in yourself and in others, you will be true leaders. If not, well, that's another story.

"So, what I want to find out is: are you really the crème de la crème, or just the cream—rich and thick?"

The students looked on transfixed, visions of their futures forming in their minds, dreaming of all the great achievements that lay ahead of them. They recalled what they had heard when they first arrived: Harvard graduates don't go looking for jobs; they create them for themselves.

As Josh listened he realized he wasn't sure what achievements he was destined for, and he wasn't sure whether fulfilment was among them. But he did feel confident that, whatever he did achieve, it would be great. He wasn't sure what his talents were, but he undoubtedly had them. It was just a process of time, of letting them mature, of slowly discovering them, and giving them the chance to develop and blossom.

The professor went on for another fifty minutes. Josh tried to follow him but, after about twenty minutes, it started to get heavy going. His pen, which at first had been busy scribbling, gradually became less active, then fell into a state of inactivity from which it never recovered. By the end, he himself had also fallen into a state of stupor. A sudden shift in tone of the professor broke him out of his lethargy.

"And that," the professor said, "is the challenge lying ahead of you." He smiled, closed down the PowerPoint, and gathered up his papers. "We will meet again next week."

The class sat there momentarily absorbed. Then they collectively switched out of their reverie, broke into conversation and started to clear up. There was the sound of shuffled papers, books being stuffed into bags and the rise of chatter.

Josh slowly packed up his things. He was still thinking about what the professor had said. Rich and thick... or destined to make the country tick. But were the two really mutually exclusive?

He packed his folder, notepad and pens into his bag and shuffled his way across the row of seats towards the exit. As he approached the large wooden doors that led out of the hall, he noticed someone holding one open for him. He stepped more quickly to take the door and barely noticed the person as he passed through. But then he turned back to say thank you.

The sight of her drew him to an instant halt, like a train carriage coming to an emergency stop. With a jolt, the fatigue from the lecture left him.

She looked like she had walked out of... a shampoo commercial. Black hair almost translucent, gold streaks at the roots. Almond eyes. A faint trace of glitter on her upper cheeks. She had a magical, ethereal look, like she had just stepped off a stage. But she was chilled as well; sweat pants, hair back, as if she had hopped up off the couch at home. He had never noticed her around campus. He stood and looked at her. For a moment, he was stupefied.

He took the door from her, his gaze transfixed. She smiled briefly, then turned, shifted her bag up onto her shoulder, and began to walk away. He stood holding the door, looking after her as she disappeared into the crowd of students pouring down the corridor.

Chapter 4

For the next few days, Josh walked around in a sweet, hallucinatory daze. Whatever the course on fulfilment was about, it seemed to have worked. He felt incredibly happy, and that was after only one session.

In his mind, he dreamed of the girl. He thought about her soft black hair, the gold streaks at the roots, and the glitter under her eyes. Who was she? Where had she come from? And how on earth had he not noticed her around campus any time over the last three years?

The class only met once a week. He would have to wait seven whole days to see her again. Those seven days passed agonizingly slowly. He crossed them off on his calendar. All the while, he tried to spot the girl around college. But she seemed to have vanished as magically as she had appeared.

When the day of the class finally came round, Josh arrived early–the first time he had been early to a class in three years. He sat at the front of the lecture theater, carefully checking every student as they came into the room. She wasn't there. Then the professor arrived, and still she wasn't there.

The professor opened his books and cleared his throat into the microphone. Then, as he was making his introductory remarks, Josh heard a sound at the door. It swung open and she dashed in. If anything, she was even more gorgeous than he remembered her. She seemed to float into the room, then slid into a seat near the entrance, as light and graceful as a gazelle.

Josh turned back to face the front. He tried to return his mind to the lecture but he couldn't concentrate. The words coming from the professor's mouth just seemed to evaporate into the air. Over the next fifty minutes, even by Josh's standards, very few notes were taken. When, at last, it came to an end, he packed away, thankful that the ordeal was over. As he made his way towards the exit, he saw the girl up ahead of him as she swung through the doors and into the hall outside.

He followed her through the theater doors, then saw her further up the corridor, walking briskly, bag slung over one shoulder. He jogged a little to catch up with her.

"Hi," he said, arriving beside her, out of breath.

She carried on walking.

"You forgot..." his mind went blank, "... you forgot to say hello."

Silence. They carried on walking. Had he *really* just said that? Possibly the worst opening gambit of all time. *Jesus.*

They continued in silence. "Sorry," she said. "I didn't realize I had to greet everyone from the course."

"That's not what I... I didn't expect... I just meant..."

Silence. They fell quiet, continued walking for a few yards. They passed through a set of double doors, then turned a corner and went down a flight of stairs.

"So," Josh said. "Perhaps we can do it now."

"Do what?"

"Say hi."

The girl pulled her bag a little further up her shoulder and quickened her pace. "Hi," she said, without breaking her stride.

"That was a pretty cool lecture," Josh said. "You know, the stuff about burgers making you unhappy in the short-term, but happy in the long-term. No, hang on, that wasn't it..."

They were outside now, passing down the steps of the lecture hall, onto the path that led across the lawn. Josh followed her, half a step behind.

As they walked, an excruciating embarrassment welled up inside him. He felt like a streaker at a football match who'd lost their bottle halfway, now considering a tactical retreat. The logical thing was just to give up, apologize for wasting her time, and say goodbye. But, somehow, he felt he'd been denied a proper go. To give up now wouldn't just be a declaration of defeat. It would be giving up without even firing a shot.

They passed the entrance to Thayer Hall. "I mean," he said, "normally I fall asleep in lectures, so the fact that I made it all the way through fully *compos mentis* was a bit of a miracle."

More silence from the girl. How could she just ignore him? Jesus, Josh thought. She had transformed from the Angel Gabriel into the Whore of Babylon, all in the space of a minute.

"Look," he said finally. "Are you going to walk along like

you've had a red-hot poker shoved up your ass, or are you going to have the decency to acknowledge that I'm actually trying to chat you up?"

The girl came to a halt. Not a screeching, brakes-slammed-at-a-red-light halt. More of a slow *OK, so you mean business* kind of halt. Josh stopped too, and he stood waiting. He half expected some kind of withering remark that would shrink him to the size of an ant.

She turned to face him. "Well, I've got to hand it to you–that was at least an original chat-up line."

They looked at each other. Normally, when girls looked at Josh, he felt them look away fairly quickly. But this time, he sensed her look at him just a moment longer, just a little more closely than before.

"Well, I've been hoping to use it on someone for quite a long time."

Another pause. The girl was still looking at him. Then, when it seemed like she had looked enough, she turned away, pushed her bag a little further up her shoulder again, and resumed walking.

"So," she said, "how come you're taking *Fulfilment 101*?"

"Oh, I'm just fascinated by the whole concept of fulfilment... you know, that we're in an age of material abundance and yet most of us are living spiritually and morally vapid lives. Yourself?"

"Just thought I could do with enlightenment on the subject, that's all."

There was a pause. They carried on walking.

Finally, she turned around and confronted him. They had passed round the back of Dudley House now and stood facing each other on the sidewalk. The traffic crawled beside them towards Harvard Square.

"Look," she said, "*are* you trying to chat me up?"

"No. God, no. I mean, hit on a girl from *Fulfilment 101*? Everyone knows that course is just full of people on therapy. Come on."

"Good. I'm glad we got that straight."

"But I would like to ask you out on a date..."

She gave a look of faux surprise. "That's pretty brazen…"

"No point messing around."

"Suppose not. So, are you asking me out or inviting me out?"

"Asking you."

"OK," she said, flicking her hair back. "Ask."

Josh began a drum roll, regretted it immediately, and abandoned it halfway. "Would you like to come out on a date with me?" he said hastily.

The girl pretended to mull it over for a moment, brow knotted in thought. "Sure," she said. "I can do that."

"I didn't ask whether you *could*. I asked whether you'd *like* to…"

She smiled, exasperated. "OK… I'd *like* to…"

"Good."

Pause. Silence. Josh just stood smiling. He could feel the hallucinatory daze engulfing him.

"So are we going to fix where and when?" she asked.

"I'll figure something out. But how about we meet at the John Harvard statue at eight on Saturday. Good?"

"Fine."

"And are you going to give me your number?"

"Well," she said, "I've already agreed to a date with you. Let's not push it *too* far."

And with that, she threw her bag behind her shoulder, gave a little smile, and started walking off across the Yard. Josh stood and watched her.

"Hang on–what's your name?"

She turned and looked at him.

"Yasmin," she called back.

Then she turned and walked away.

Chapter 5

"I told you I hadn't lost the touch…"

"I cannot believe that…"

"After only five minutes…"

"Tell me you're lying…"

"Do I ever lie?"

"You're a lucky bastard…"

"You'll just have to admit it: Josh's back in the game."

"Game my ass. Total fluke. And anyway, I've never seen her around. She can't be that special."

Josh, Louis and Zak sat around the dining table of Adams House. In the dark, wooden interior, students emerged from the canteen with trays piled high with food. Louis was in his usual Harvard mascot outfit, muscles glistening from lifting his own body weight several thousand times in the gym. Zak couldn't smoke indoors, so he toyed with his rolling papers and lighter, and looked at his plate of rice and lentils quizzically.

"For Christ's sake, Zak, it's a plate of food, not a riddle. Just eat it. Anyway," said Louis, turning back to Josh, "talk me through it one more time."

"We were coming out of the lecture theater. She was looking all stuffy and unapproachable. I jogged up to her with the worst line ever. Then, with my natural verve and winning charm, I rescued the situation, and made myself appear totally *irresistible*."

"Well, I bet that's not the whole story. But I've got to hand it to you. One moment rejected and spurned, next moment you bounce back like a squash ball. Respect to you, lad. I'm impressed." Louis punched Zak. "That's impressive, isn't it, Zak?"

Zak broke off from his reverie. "I'm sorry? Yes, yes, of course. That's extraordinary. Really… extraordinary."

"It *is* extraordinary," said Louis. "So anyway, where are you taking her?"

"Not sure yet."

"Not sure? Come on, my boy. You better think, and quick.

Saturday is just around the corner. What are your options?"

"Well, there's that dessert place that's opened up…"

"That's lame," Louis said. "You can't take a girl out just for dessert."

"Or the Hong Kong…"

"A heady cocktail of noodle soup and tequila…."

"Or of course there's one of the Final Clubs," Josh said.

"There are worse places to go. Know of any parties going down?"

"I'd need to make some inquiries."

"I heard a rumor that *United Acapella* were doing a beer pong competition…"

"Bit messy… in multiple ways…"

Zak turned to them. "The *Signet Society* are doing a costume party. Famous psychoanalytic case histories."

"God, *that* sounds fun…"

"Or, if you want to really impress her," Louis said, "the *Phoenix* are throwing a two halves party."

"What do you mean?"

"You know… come as one half, and you find your other half."

"No way…"

"Yes, way. And rumor is, it's going to be *massive*."

Pause.

"So, you want me to get you in there?" Louis said.

"Is it possible?"

"Josh, my lad, anything is possible when Louis is around. Ain't that right, Zak?" He slapped Zak heavily, his palm crashing down on his back like a breaking wave. Zak dropped his rolling papers and looked up. "Oh yes, sorry, yes… of course… that's right."

Louis leaned forward and looked at Josh intently. "Josh, with the powers invested in me as the fairy godmother of your social life, I hereby pronounce that you *will* go to the ball on Saturday night, in the company of your beautiful new romantic interest. You *will* seduce her with your unwavering charm, and may only good things come of it."

"Zak," he said, leaning back and putting his arm around him, "be a good fellow and run to the dessert counter. I could really use some more ice-cream.”

***

The next two days passed slowly. In classes, Josh gazed into space. There were no more *Fulfilment 101* lectures until next week so he wouldn’t see Yasmin again until Saturday night. Until then, he just had to wait.

When Saturday arrived, Josh spent the day scouring the secondhand shops of Cambridge for outfits. After hours of searching, he had still drawn a blank. But finally, in desperation, he bought a pair of aviators–a gesture towards Maverick from *Top Gun*–and something for Yasmin as well.

After dinner he jogged down the stone steps from his hall of residence. The evenings were warm enough that the Yard gently hummed with activity; groups of students sat on dorm porches and out on the lawns, lazing around in clusters, playing guitars, wandering the streets in inebriated gaggles. Cherry blossom hung in the trees and dusted the sidewalks all around.

He made his way through the Yard and there she was, where she said she would be, by the John Harvard statue, wearing a white, summery dress. They greeted one another with a kiss on the cheek then stood back to look at each other.

“Why are you wearing those ridiculous glasses?” she said.

“Oh yeah, I forgot to say: we’re going to a costume party.”

“Please tell me you’re joking.”

“Nope…”

“What kind of costume party?”

“Two halves–come as one half, you have to discover your other half.”

“Right. And you’ve come as?”

“Well…” Josh flicked down his aviators. Yasmin groaned.

“Come on. Greatest ‘80s romance *ever*.”

She frowned. “But what about me?”

“I brought you something.” He handed her a yellow cardigan.

“What’s this?”

“Think…”

“No movie heroines wear yellow cardigans.”

21

"Think harder. And here's a clue: you just happen to be wearing a white dress, which is perfect."

She continued to think. "No…"

"*Oh Danny*," Josh said, grief-stricken, in a passable Australian accent.

"Sandy in *Grease*?"

"You got it."

"But, where are the black leggings? The red shoes?"

"I was going to bring those. Wasn't sure what size you were though…"

"Maybe that's just as well. Wouldn't want to look *too* nice. It'll probably be one of those parties where you get covered in beer."

"Not all Final Clubs parties are like that."

Pause. They looked at each other. Josh felt reassured. She had been a bit scary the first time they had met. Now she seemed to have softened a bit. He felt his heart beat a little slower and his body relax.

"Come on," he said. "Let's see if Charlie and Danny are waiting for us somewhere."

Walking through the Yard, they passed people already well on their way, lurching drunkenly in black tie along the paths. They walked down Holyoke Street, then right along Mount Auburn until they arrived at an austere doorway. Standing at the enormous entrance, it sounded fairly quiet within. There was just a faint, audible murmur of conversation.

Yasmin looked uncertain. "You sure this is the place? It's very quiet."

He reached up and rang the bell.

"Josh, if you've dragged me out for no reason…"

At last, they heard a sound from inside, the click of a latch being opened, and the door swung open. A young man stood on the other side. He looked like a typical preppy Ivy-Leaguer in beige chinos, a pastel-pink *Ralph Lauren* sweater over a light blue shirt, and a tie loose around his neck.

"Evening. You on the guest list?"

"I think so. Josh Mayhew, plus one."

He scrolled down the checklist. "Yes," he said, ticking them off. He looked up and smiled. "Come on in."

They stepped across the threshold and went inside. Josh expected all the hallmarks of a frat party; hysterical games of beer pong, girls draped over banisters, sweaty jocks heaving around, baseball caps worn backwards. But there was none of that. All he could see were a few nerdy kids sipping from plastic cups.

Guarding a keg in the corner, a custodial student carefully dispensed beer through a hose. Josh and Yasmin each filled a red plastic cup, stood back to drink, and surveyed the scene.

"So," he said, "I didn't have a chance to talk to you properly that day."

"Sorry. I was in a hurry."

"How you finding the class?"

"I really like it. You?"

"Honestly? Dull as hell."

"No…"

"Afraid so. Ironic, in a course on fulfilment."

"Why?" she said.

"Well, I quite like being a hedonist. But he said in the first lecture that wasn't a recipe for happiness. It's suited me quite nicely…"

"Maybe not in the long-term."

"But there *is* no long-term…"

He smiled and, a moment later, she smiled too. They paused for more swigs of beer.

"Anyway, where are you from?" she asked. "I can't figure out your accent."

"New Jersey."

"Local boy."

"Yeah, i.e. lazy. Couldn't be bothered to travel far. Plus my parents didn't want me out of their eyesight. You?"

"LA."

"Oh. You must be suffering."

"Yeah. The winters are brutal. I have to fight the urge to flee each time November rolls around. But I kind of like having seasons for a change."

They took another couple of swigs of beer, draining their cups.

"Another one?" Josh said.

Yasmin frowned. "Are you trying to get me drunk?"

"God, no. Do I look like I could carry you home?"

"Oi," she said, punching him.

The party was finally starting to get lively. Away in a far corner, a centurion drinking contest was taking place; they'd only reached forty but two people had already passed out. More people had arrived in costume. Across the room, Josh could spot several people dressed as Batman (and a few as Robin). There was the odd black-suited Vincent Vega and Jules Winnfield, and a few Thelma and Louises, too.

"You know," Josh said, "about what we were saying–if you really want to find out who the happiest people in the world are, there's only one way to find out…"

"Oh, yeah? What's that?"

"Hit the dance floor."

"What do you mean?"

"The happiest people shine on the dance floor."

"Oh no…"

"Come on…"

"I'm not big on dancing…"

"Come on," he said, walking off.

"You won't get me…"

"It's the only way to decide…"

He put his cup down on a table and headed across the room. She followed reluctantly. Out the door, they walked up a grand carpeted staircase. The walls were decorated with wooden sporting plaques, stuffed bison and deer heads, trophies, and photos of handsome, clean-shaven, waspy young men in blazers.

Upstairs, they emerged into a large room. It was the dance floor, and it was completely empty.

"Wow," Josh said. "There's nothing like having a dance floor completely to yourself."

As they began walking across, thin streams of green neon light filtered through onto the floor. The sound system was already on and a generic *Motown* all-time greatest hits playlist was blasting out. Josh took out his phone, scanned through his tracks and plugged it in.

"OK," he said. "First up, how about this?"

The jaunty sound of Chuck Berry's *You Never Can Tell* played over the system. They danced, slightly self-consciously at first, avoiding looking in each other's eyes.

The track came to an end. "OK," Yasmin said. "My choice now." She skimmed through his songs, hit play and put the phone down. Josh listened to the opening notes–the strains of a saxophone against a plucked guitar.

"Don't recognize it," he said.

"Come on," she said. "*Baby I Love Your Way*. '90s classic."

They danced again, more silly and relaxed this time, swaying to the reggae beat. By the end of the song, they were comfortably gyrating next to each other.

"Well," Josh said as it came to an end, "if we're heading down that path, there's only one option."

He skimmed through some more tracks on his phone, then triumphantly hit the play button. A bass-baritone voice sounded over the system.

"*Dirty Dancing*," Yasmin groaned. "Talk about the cheesiest song *ever*."

As the beat quickened, Josh took her in his arms, planting his right hand on her back and taking her right hand in his left. They began to waltz around the room, revolving in circles. She avoided eye contact, casting her eyes away to the floor, and then away from him again as they changed direction.

"You know," he said, "I was junior ballroom dancing champion of New Jersey."

"I would never have guessed."

She smiled, looked into his eyes for a moment, then cast her gaze away.

The song came to an end. They stopped and stood in the middle of the dance floor. Except for the distant hum of conversation from downstairs, everything was quiet. He looked down into her eyes and she looked back at him, the glitter on her cheeks catching the light.

He felt her hands extend around his back. He closed his eyes and felt the breath from her mouth on his cheek, then the touch of her lips against his.

She whispered something but Josh couldn't hear it properly.
"I'm sorry?" he said.
"*Jigareto bokhoram.*"
"I don't…"
"It's… don't worry."
He opened his eyes and stood back to look at her.
"Tell me."
"*Jigareto bokhoram.*"
"What language is that?"
"It's Persian…"
"And it means?"
"Literally, *I want to eat your liver.*"
Josh let go of her and took a step back.
"You *what*?"
"I want to eat your liver."
"Well, *that's* an original one…"
"Yeah, it's a bit weird…"
"Yikes. Slightly scary. I thought for a moment you'd morphed into Hannibal Lector–that you were about to sink your teeth into my neck and make up for missing breakfast…"
"No, no, you're safe. For the time being. It's just an expression. If you like someone, you like their liver."
"Right."
"And if you *really* like someone…"
"You want to eat it. OK. Thanks for explaining. Well, I kind of need my liver. And most of my other organs. But if I think of any I don't need, I'll call up the Yasmin food bank."
"Much appreciated."
Pause. They stood smiling at each other.
"Anyway, what language did you say that was?"
"Persian."
"Right. And they speak that in…?"
"Iran. But I'm not Iranian. Well, I'm not from there. I grew up in LA."
"So what makes you–"
"Iranian? My parents are." She sighed. "I've never even been."
"But you'd like to?"

"Like to? I'd love to. But it's not safe…"

"How come?"

"Oh, issues with my family. Boring stuff. But it's my country, you know. It's part of me."

They stood for a moment longer. Then, suddenly, a wave of agitation seemed to sweep over Yasmin's face. She looked away.

"What's wrong?"

"Nothing…"

"You look distracted."

"No, it's nothing."

"Sure?"

She sighed, looked down at the floor, then up at him.

"Look, I probably shouldn't be doing this."

"What?"

"This…"

"Coming to a debauched Final Club…"

"No… *this*," she said gesturing to the space between them. She stood back and looked at him, then looked down at the floor, and sighed again.

"I've got a boyfriend, Josh. Not here. Back in LA."

"Well, that's OK…"

"No, it's not OK. I love him. And if he could see me now… look… I think we better end the evening here. Alright?" She looked him in the eye. "I'm sorry. It's been a really lovely night."

She held his gaze a moment longer, then put one hand on his chest, palm down on the front of his jacket, stood on her tiptoes, and moved her other hand up over his shoulder and around the back of his neck. She brought her face up close to his. He dipped his head and turned it to the side so her mouth was against his ear.

"You're lovely, but I think we met at the wrong time." She brushed her mouth against his cheek–not a kiss, just a slight linger–then she slowly took it away.

She lowered herself off her toes, looked up at him one more time, then turned and began to walk away. Josh stayed with his head dipped, motionless on the dance floor. He stayed there until

the touch of her mouth on his cheek was no longer a feeling but
a memory.

Chapter 6

For the next few weeks, Josh didn't see Yasmin. *Fulfilment 101* now consisted of seminars, so he didn't see her at the lecture theater.

Sometimes he meandered around campus on the off-chance that he would catch sight of her. Or he would sit at his desk in the library, staring out the window at the figures walking across the lawns, searching for her in the crowds. But there was no sign of her. He often found his mind wandering back to that night at the Final Club; the dancing, the kiss… the boyfriend.

All this time, he thought about what she'd said. *Jigareto bokhoram.* What kind of culture promotes human liver consumption? That was definitely weird. The closest he'd come to deviant behavior was getting a henna tattoo of a scorpion when he was fifteen, and he had to be honest, that wasn't exactly 'out there'. Liver consumption, on the other hand, definitely was. But, at the same time, he did find the idea intriguing, even faintly seductive. Not the actual thought of having his organs eaten. It was just such a different way of expressing affection. Josh had spent the whole of his life in New Jersey. Sure, his friends were a mix of backgrounds. But actually, all his (short-lived) girlfriends had been pretty similar to him. Yasmin was different. And somehow that felt good.

But the real thing that preoccupied him was something else. Los Angeles. California.

Josh had never been to the West Coast. But ever since his first viewing of *Baywatch* as a teenager, he had vivid images of it in his head; palm trees swaying against a deep-blue sky, bronzed torsos, life-size Barbie dolls in orange swimsuits, wooden huts on stilts with floats hanging outside them. The more he thought about them, the more he couldn't get those images out of his mind. Soon, everywhere he went, he saw traces of them; the lawns on campus turned into sand beneath his feet and there were moments when he looked up and saw not the dull clouds of Massachusetts, but the vast, blue Californian sky, stretched out above his head.

Spring turned into summer and soon it was graduation time. A sense of relief spread through college now the pressure of exams had lifted, like the gentle deflation of an overfilled balloon. Festivities and celebrations filled the air. There were garden parties that carried on all afternoon and, as the days grew longer, people became nocturnal and spent their evenings sitting out on the lawns.

Then came *Commencement*. Campus was filled with students in gowns, beaming and slightly overwhelmed. Parents converged on town, fussing proudly over their offspring. Josh's did too, driving up from New Jersey for the occasion. They passed the day going through the usual formalities: drinks receptions, speeches, photos on the footsteps of all the buildings, goodbyes, endless wishes of good luck.

His parents drove home that night. After seeing them off, he walked home alone. He was exhausted; he hadn't slept the night before and, as he walked, he felt light-headed and vacant. Dusk was falling and he felt his body weighed down by the heavy gown, his feet aching from standing all day.

He stood waiting at a crossing on Mount Auburn Street. Then, up ahead of him, he saw a figure he recognized. He narrowed his eyes to make out who it was. Yasmin. She was coming towards him on the opposite side. He checked for traffic and crossed the road to meet her.

"Yasmin."

"Josh."

They stood on the sidewalk facing each other. She had changed out of her graduation gown and was wearing jeans and a T-shirt, a bag slung over her shoulder.

"How are you?" he said.

"I'm good. Yourself?"

"Yeah, I'm fine."

There was a slight pause as they looked at each other hesitantly, wondering who would speak next.

"Good graduation?" he said.

"Not bad. How about you?"

"It was OK. My jaw aches from smiling so much. And I feel like I've said enough goodbyes to last a lifetime. But apart from that, good."

Another pause. A car passed by. Slight embarrassment now, the initial enthusiasm upon seeing each other giving way to awkwardness.

"So," she said, "what are your plans now? Heading off somewhere exciting?"

"No, sadly not. You?"

"I'm going traveling."

"Yeah?"

"Discover myself. I've spent the last few years stuck in the library. I need to go and learn what the real world is like."

"Where are you going?"

"The standard. Round-the-world trip..."

"And Iran?"

"No. There are–"

"Issues with your family. I remember."

"Yeah. It's just Europe. Inter-railing. Some of the Middle East. Then India, Southeast Asia... the obvious, I guess. Frolicking with elephants and tigers. Make love to the earth. That kind of thing."

"By yourself?"

"No..." She hesitated. "With..."

"Your boyfriend. Sorry."

"So... what about you? You're not leaving town?"

"Not sure. I haven't made plans yet."

"You better decide quickly. You don't want to hang around Boston in the summer. It turns into a swamp."

"I know. Maybe I'll head off somewhere."

"Right..."

"Go on some kind of adventure..."

"OK..."

"Maybe," he said, a thought suddenly coming into his head. "Maybe I'll go to LA."

"LA?"

"Yeah."

"How come?"

"I don't know. Just to bask in the sunshine. Or rot in the cultural desert. Whichever comes easiest."

"Well, you might like it…"

"Because it's a cultural desert?"

"Because of the sunshine. It'll help your pasty complexion."

"Hey…"

"Just kidding."

They fell into silence. She looked up at him. "Well, I better be going. I've got to see my parents off to the airport." She smiled. "It was nice seeing you."

"Nice seeing you, too."

"Keep in touch."

"Yes. Keep me informed while you're on the road. Send me a postcard through *Facebook*. Does *Facebook* do that? They should. If not, at least poke me from time to time to let me know you're still alive."

"OK. But, don't worry. You'll know I'm still alive from all the hysterical updates about every tiny thing I see while I'm away."

"I promise to read every word."

"Er, please *don't*…"

They smiled.

"Well," she said. "Take care of yourself."

"You too."

There was a pause, each of them unsure how to end it appropriately. After a moment, they spontaneously moved into a hug. Josh put his arms around her and he felt her do the same. They held it for a moment, then they gently let go and stood back.

Then she smiled, turned, and walked away up the sidewalk.

Josh stood for a moment, savoring the summer evening air. Then he started walking back towards his apartment. As he walked, he thought about what he'd said. California. He'd never even considered going there until now. It was just a random idea that had popped into his head, like a fly buzzing from nowhere into his field of vision.

He thought about it more as he walked back home. He was still thinking about it as he unlocked the front door of his apartment. Still doing so as he took off his gown and shoes, and flung them on the couch. Then, moments later, he was upstairs, on his computer, booking a flight to LA.

Chapter 7

Josh had four days to catch up with his decision. He frantically packed up his belongings, giving away unneeded things on *Freecycle*, cramming storage items into plastic boxes, smiling sycophantically at friends, and asking if he could 'temporarily' leave them in their basements. He managed to shed most of the clutter he had accumulated over four years but, the day he left Boston, he ended up with a pile heaped on the sidewalk, to which passersby could help themselves.

He crammed everything he needed into two massive suitcases. Heaving them through Cambridge, he felt like a body-snatcher lugging two corpses. Reaching the Square, he stood waiting for the airport bus. It was a mid-summer evening but, as he stood on the sidewalk, the subway entrance sent up gusts of cool air. He shivered and felt the goose pimples rise on his arms.

He tried to read on the flight but, instead, he spent most of the time gazing out the window, looking at the empty stretches of land below. As they flew west, the landscape grew darker, the clusters of orange lights further and further apart. By the time they began the descent into LA, it was night. The city seemed to stretch out to infinity. In every direction, all he could see was row upon row of gridded orange lights. The air was foggy and misty, and there was a haze hanging over the land. It made the lights below twinkle and blur, like he was looking down on some vast civilization from the future.

Passing through baggage reclaim, he wheeled his trolley towards the exit, through a series of automatic doors, and finally from the air-conditioned arrivals hall out into the taxi depot. The nighttime warmth was smothering, engulfing him seductively, like a dressing gown after a shower. He took a deep breath and felt a thrill of excitement. He wanted to bellow *"Hello, California,"* the way presenters do at awards ceremonies, but he just said it quietly to himself in his head.

He stood at the curb, savoring the air amid the taxi depot commotion. Then, cutting through the noise, came a shout.

"Need a ride?"

He dropped out of his reverie and pushed his trolley over to the cab waiting by the curb. The driver lifted his bags into the trunk and Josh got in the back seat, the door closing with a thud.

"Venice, please. Cabrillo Avenue."

They set off slowly, gathering speed as they passed through a maze of twisting concrete ramps, then emerging suddenly onto the freeway, shooting out like a dart into the LA night. As they coasted along, Josh pressed his face against the window and stared out at the jungle of concrete blocks and palm trees silhouetted against the night sky.

"New to LA?"

Josh glanced forward. The driver was looking at him through the rearview mirror.

"Yes."

Josh returned his gaze to the road. The driver looked at the freeway ahead.

"What brings you here?"

"Oh, nothing much."

There was a pause. The driver smiled. "That's what they all say. Don't wanna build their hopes up. Everyone comes here for something, man."

"No," Josh said. "There's nothing."

"You wanna act. You wanna write. You're a musician. Something."

"No, really..."

They fell into silence. The driver looked at the road ahead.

"Maybe it's a girl..." The driver looked up at him through the mirror. Josh could feel his stare coming back at him.

"No," Josh said, "it's nothing like that." He turned back to face the window.

They fell into silence and continued along the freeway. A few minutes passed, no one saying anything.

"So," the driver said after a while, "where you gonna be living? Venice?"

"At first. While I look for somewhere long-term."

"Oh, yeah? Where you gonna look?"

"Don't know," Josh said. Then something flitted into his mind. "Hey," he said, leaning forward. "Could you tell me something… do you know many Iranians here?"

The driver paused. "*Eye-ranians?*"

"Yes."

The driver looked puzzled, thinking to himself for a moment. "You mean, *Persians*?"

"No… Iranians."

The driver looked in his mirror and changed lanes. "No, I don't. I know Koreans. I know Armenians. I know little Saigon. I know little Ethiopia. But I don't know any Iranians."

Josh settled back in his seat. "Which part of town are you from?"

"Hollywood," the driver said. "The north part." He paused for a moment. "It's where dreams are made. And where dreams are shattered."

Josh turned back to face out the window. They spent the rest of the journey in silence, the driver with his eyes on the road, Josh with his face against the window.

A short while later, they pulled up at the house in Venice. Painted bright purple and blue, merging into the dark, it was a lonely building on a street of warehouses. The driver got out and heaved the bags from the trunk. Josh paid the fare then stood on the sidewalk as the driver walked back round to the front of the car. He opened the door then stopped. He looked at Josh across the roof.

"Look," he said, "you've only just arrived here. So I'm going to give you some advice. It may not come in handy but, on the other hand, it might. Remember, LA is a jungle. And I don't know about the Iranians, but if I had to guess, I'd say they're part of the jungle as well."

He looked at Josh one last time, then ducked his head, got into the car and turned on the ignition. There was a pause while the engine ran, then the car purred off, like a cat in the night.

Josh stood on the sidewalk, his bags beside him. He watched as the car disappeared slowly down the street. Through the warm, dusky air, he could hear the sound of the ocean, distant but heavy. Everything else was silent and still.

Chapter 8

He woke early the next morning, his face warmed by the sun streaming through the skylight above his head. Bright, luminescent rays filled the room.

His friend Alexis had said he could crash with her for a few days. Alexis had been a friend since high school. Skipping college, she had gone straight out to California to find work in the movies. She now spent most of her time dressed up in a giant bunny outfit trying to lure tourists into gift shops on Hollywood Boulevard.

As he lay in bed, he still wasn't quite sure what he was doing in LA. But he knew that, whatever the situation, there was one thing he needed to do fast: find a place to live. Alexis and he were close, but not so close that he could stay with her indefinitely. She'd said 'fine' when he asked to stay. But a couple of days *maximum*. After that, he was on his own.

So he set to work trawling through the room ads online. He began the process hopefully. But, as he read on, his optimism faded. They all sounded so… *weird*. "No smoking or drugs including alcohol on the premises. I need quiet during the day for long periods of Tibetan Buddhist meditation and yoga." "Spiritual practitioner looking for enlightened housemate… I want to live with someone who can help me discover resonance with my orgasmic inner being." Josh liked the idea of different lifestyles but this was a step too far. Each ad seemed to go further into some alternative reality of spiritual mumbo jumbo.

The morning of the third day, he got a text from Alexis. *Josh,* it said, *been lovely having you, but you can't stay any longer. A friend's got a space in her apartment. She can take you from now on. She'll be over at nine. Make sure you've got your stuff packed. Good luck!*

Josh looked at his watch. It was 9:00 a.m. and, sure enough, the doorbell rang.

On the front doorstep stood a formidable-looking woman–a sort of combination of Barbie doll and nightclub bouncer. She wore stiletto heels, had peroxide blonde hair and sunglasses perched on top of her coiffured hairdo. At the same time, she had a robust, trunk-like body, with a stance like a football player, suggesting a possible past life as a body-builder. If he'd encountered her in a back alley, he would have quickened his stride.

She looked squarely at him. "Josh?"

"Yes."

"Friend of Alexis?"

"Yes."

"Come," she said, with unquestionable authority.

"Where are we…?"

"Where are your things?"

"OK… hang on."

Josh dashed back into the house, crammed his stuff into his bags and lugged them down to the sidewalk. The woman picked them up, one in each hand, and took them down to an open-top silver *Mercedes*. Josh followed behind.

"Can I just ask," he said, getting into the car behind her and throwing a few last garments into the back, "where we're going?"

"Don't worry," the woman said, expressionless, but also with a hint of 'time is money'.

With Josh in the back seat, they set off. She seemed to know the city well, avoiding all the main roads, taking only side-alleys and back-routes. As they drove, Josh reached back, wind whooshing past his ears, splaying his arms out over his belongings to keep them from blowing away. At first, he tried to follow where they were going, but he soon gave up.

"So," he shouted from the back seat. "What's your name?"

"Niki."

"And, what do you do Niki?"

Niki shrugged. "This and that."

"Fashion?" She was well-dressed, in a shoulder-padded power suit.

"A little."

"TV?" Perhaps she was an agent, Josh thought. She had that pushy look about her.

"Sometimes."

"Movies…?"

Niki raised her hand and wiggled it from side to side. "Sort of."

They continued through the backstreets. Then finally, after a giddy succession of U-turns, screechy corners and fractional shaves with car wing mirrors, they pulled up at an apartment block. Josh felt like he'd been blindfolded, spun about, and put in a wind tunnel, but now he looked around and breathed a sigh of relief. The streets were wide, the lawns were green and the palm trees rose high into the sky. A calm descended upon him. It was as close as you could get to his vision of quintessential LA.

Niki must have seen the relief in his face. "Don't worry," she said. "Beverly Hills. A good area."

She strode round to the back of the car and plucked his bags out of the trunk. Josh took them and heaved them up the front steps of the building. Inside, they took the elevator to the third floor. They walked a little way down the corridor, then Niki opened a door into an apartment. Josh followed her through and looked around.

Inside the apartment was, well, if he had to use one word: hideous. It was thickly carpeted, but not with the elegant designs he usually saw in the carpet shops in New York. The colors were crude–almost hallucinogenic. Dotted around were strange spooky sculptures; Josh didn't know much about art, but they looked like Indian deities, with flailing arms and bulging eyes. On the walls were large abstract paintings with big splashes of garish paint.

"Make yourself at home," Niki said.

Josh looked around uncertainly.

"You can use that mattress on the floor."

He stood and assessed his situation. It wasn't ideal. But when it came to the crunch, he was homeless. It would have to do.

"Right," he said. "We better talk about money."

Niki waved her hand. "Not important."

"What's the arrangement though?"

"Don't worry," Niki said.

"But how much–"

"We'll settle on something."

"Niki, I'd prefer it if we agreed a price–"

But she was already picking up her bag and preparing to leave. She took her keys from the side table. "I'll call you," she said, the way you say goodbye to someone at the end of an awful first date whom you never want to see again. And then she was gone.

Josh stood in the middle of the room and looked around. He looked at the paintings. He felt the gaze of the grinning statues. After a while, he felt like he was being watched. He felt a nauseous wave building up in him, then he went over to the bed, closed his eyes, and tried to shut out everything around him.

Chapter 9

Josh spent the following days wandering the streets of Beverly Hills. Walking along the wide boulevards, he happily absorbed the rays of sun that flooded the streets. It was even more glorious than he had imagined. The sidewalks were flanked by perfect, tall palm trees, in stately processional formation either side of the road. Their slender trunks reached high into the sky, disappearing into the heavens like fairytale beanstalks, so far up you had to squint to see their tops. Down below at ground level were houses of every imaginable design; mock Tudor, Italianate villas, French châteaus, each presented with a subtle yet distinctly noticeable sign for a private security firm on its front lawn. But, the weird thing was, there were no pedestrians. The only sign of life came from the constant hum of hedge trimmers and the sight of an occasional gardener vacuuming leaves, emptying bins or pruning hedges.

One evening, Josh arrived back at the apartment exhausted. He had been walking all day and his legs felt like lead weights. He collapsed onto his mattress on the floor, put the air-conditioning on full blast, and lay under the cool stream of air. The goose pimples rose on his skin and he felt a pleasing shiver from the cold.

Then he heard a sound from the entrance. He turned to see Niki coming through the door. He was accustomed to her brief visits, or, 'checking the apartment because she might have people moving in'. But she had agreed to shelter him until that happened and, in the meantime, he would find somewhere permanent to live.

"Inspection," she announced.

He looked across at her from his position on the bed.

"I may have people moving in," she said. "Need to check everything is ready."

Josh lay on the bed as Niki went around the apartment checking things. She inspected the walls and window frames, searching for imperfections. She ran her fingers over the paintwork to check for dust. She went into the kitchen to carry on her examination, but Josh knew there was something she wanted to tell him because she kept stealing glances over at him. Finally, she spoke.

"Josh," she said, peering at the kitchen sideboard, "you seem to have a problem with the heat."

Josh lay on the mattress and didn't say anything.

"You're always sweating."

Josh remained silent.

"You know why?" Niki said.

"No."

"Because you are over-heating."

Josh turned over on the bed, facing up towards the ceiling. Niki continued her inspection.

"You know, some people might call that a problem." Niki was looking through the kitchen cupboards now. A few moments passed, then she spoke again.

"And what is this you're eating?"

"What?"

"All this."

"That's spaghetti."

"Well it's a lot. You have a big appetite."

"That's because I have a high metabolism."

"Maybe. Or perhaps," she said, "there is something wrong."

"I don't think there's anything wrong," Josh said, closing his eyes now.

"Maybe," Niki shifted her attention away from the cupboard and turned to face him, "you have a *condition*."

"I don't have a condition."

"I think maybe you do."

"Like what?"

Niki looked at him gravely. "Hyper-thyroidism."

"*Hyper-thyroidism*?"

"Yes. Hyper-thyroidism. It has two symptoms. Over-heating and over-eating. You've got both."

Josh lay on his bed on the floor and Niki resumed her inspection. After a few moments, she came into the sitting room and sat on the couch opposite him. He felt her give him a long, inquisitive look.

"Josh, I hope you don't mind me asking, but what exactly are you doing in LA?"

"I told you before."

Niki nodded slowly, but she still looked puzzled.

"OK. So you've just graduated, but what are you going to do now you're here? I mean, where are you going to live?"

"Maybe I can find a family to live with or something."

"You want to live with a family?"

"Yes."

"What makes you think you can do that?"

"Well, it would be a good way of experiencing the city, connecting with people. You know."

"Well, yes. But you think you can do this in LA?"

"Maybe."

Niki gave him a concerned look and leaned towards him. "Josh. There is something you must know. This is LA. This is not a city where you find some family to take you in. Here, you are by yourself."

Josh lay still for a moment and thought about this. "OK," he said. "So maybe I won't find a family to live with. But I will at least find somewhere to live."

Niki nodded. "And what will you do once you have found a place to live?"

"Find a job."

"And then?"

"Make some friends."

"And then?"

"*I* don't know…"

"Well, you better–"

"I don't know," he said exasperatedly. "Does it matter?"

They fell silent. Niki sat on the couch looking at him.

"Josh," she said after a while. "I am worried that you don't understand Los Angeles."

"What do you mean?"

"Los Angeles, you know, it's not an easy city. You need some kind of plan. I mean, to start, how will you get around?"

"By bike."

"I'm sorry?"

"Bike. I like cycling. I've always cycled."

Niki sighed. "OK. Rule number one: you need a car. You can try your bike, but you won't get very far."

"We'll see. I've cycled in every other city I've lived in."

"Yes, we'll see. Now, rule two: watch your back. LA is a crazy city. It's like… a wild jungle. You must be careful. Many people will try to… *screw* you over."

"Niki, I think you're exaggerating…"

"No, I'm not. Please be careful."

"OK, I'll be careful."

"Good. When I came here, I was like you. I thought I could do things my way. But I learned that life is more complicated than that."

Josh lay where he was and stared at the ceiling. After a while, he turned to face her.

"When did you come to LA, Niki?"

"A long time ago."

"When?"

"Probably before you were born."

Josh looked at her. He found this hard to believe. Niki was a fair bit older than him, but she couldn't be *that* much older.

"How old were you when you came?"

"I was a little girl," she said.

"And where did you grow up?"

"In Iran."

Josh sat up in bed. He looked at her properly now. He didn't know what Iranian women looked like. But something told him Niki wasn't a typical Iranian woman. The blond hair. The mini skirt. The high heels. Somehow she didn't seem to fit.

"When I was in Iran, I was very different to how I am now," she said, sensing what he was thinking.

She smiled to herself, as if she were surprised at such a thing. But, after a moment, she snapped out of it. "Anyway, that's another story." She stood up, went back into the kitchen, performing a final check on the fridge.

Josh lay back down on the bed, staring up at the ceiling.

"Niki," he said, "nothing bad is going to happen to me. I'm just an innocent guy who's come to LA. That's all. I'm not going to have any trouble. Trust me.”

Josh remained lying on the bed staring at the ceiling. Then he started to sense the paintings again. The weird sculptures with their garish colors and spooky grins. Down in his stomach, he could sense a sick feeling. But this time, it was more than just sickness. It was a feeling of dread. It seemed to build up inside him, from his stomach, slowly rising like some foul gas creeping up to the surface of a swamp. He closed his eyes and tried not to think about anything.

Chapter 10

Josh spent the next few weeks in Niki's apartment. As each day passed, the sense of desperation grew inside him. He couldn't just live on someone's floor indefinitely like some kind of parasitic house guest. He would have to find a place of his own. And anyway, Niki had said she had people moving in. If he didn't find somewhere soon, she would throw him out and he would be left scrounging favors, in a city where he didn't even know anyone to scrounge favors off.

He continued to scan the *Craigslist* ads. He left messages. He went to viewings. But all the people he met made him feel uncomfortable. They all seemed a bit unhinged; delusional writers, desperate hopefuls, day-dreamers trying to make it big in Hollywood. After a while, it became depressing. Of course, he recognized himself as a bit of a loser. But there was nothing like being surrounded by others in the same predicament to magnify the feeling. It was like looking in a mirror and seeing a thousand of yourself staring back at you.

One morning, when he could feel the desperation building to a peak, there came a sliver of hope. His response to a free room in Brentwood yielded a reply. He sensed that this might be the final roll of the dice.

Journeying over to the Westside, he sat on the bus as it wound its way up the hills, through the long, gently curving, tree-lined streets. They grew quieter as they left the main road behind. He got off and walked the last bit. Walking uphill, all he could hear was the sound of his shoes on the gravel along the edge of the asphalt and birdsong coming from the trees.

Finally, towards the top of the hill, where the road fizzled out and the trees and foliage took over, he arrived at the address. A two-story rambling mansion, it felt like an archaeological site–a kind of ancient Mayan ruin in the jungle. The path to the front door was lined with cacti and behind them grew a tangle of vines, gigantic ferns and winding creepers. The growth was so thick you could hardly see the building behind and, where it did appear, it seemed to grow out of the plants, like it had come into a symbiotic relationship with its surroundings.

Josh began to walk up the garden path. Then, as he approached the building, he heard a wheezing sound. He paused to listen. Again it came: a wheeze, then the sound of high-pitched laughter.

He peered through the foliage. Following the direction of the noise, he pushed aside a couple of ferns and began to pass through the undergrowth. Then, after a few meters, he came to a clearing. In the middle, there was a man sitting cross-legged and bare-chested. He was sharply taking in air, pausing, and then emitting a hysterical laugh. Josh stood watching for a moment. He was just about to interrupt when the man opened his eyes.

"Woah," he said, coiling back with surprise.

"Sorry to disturb…"

"You gave me a fright…"

"I'm Josh. We spoke about the room?"

The man stood up and stuck out a hand.

"Nima," he said. "You scared the hell out of me there."

They shook hands. Nima looked like a hermit who had just returned from years spent in the desert, or a new-age version of those early Christian ascetics who lived on columns. He wore Bermuda shorts, red flip flops and a colorful open Hawaiian shirt. He had a ponytail and a goatee beard. His face was wizened from many hours spent in the sun and he had piercing dark-brown eyes.

"Laughter yoga," Nima said. "Keeps the lungs in shape." He picked up the yoga mat that he had been sitting on. "Come on. I'll show you the house."

Nima parted the ferns and Josh followed him through the thick undergrowth up to the house. Through the front door, they passed into the cool, dark interior. From the outside, the house had looked like a ruin. Inside, it was like a ruin, too. Paint was peeling off the walls and a thick layer of dust covered everything. It was quiet, with a damp, musty smell, like being at the bottom of a rainforest.

They passed through the house. The walls and ceiling were painted in a swirling black and white design that evoked the swill and churn of the ocean. The whole place was crammed full of clutter: enormous ferns, antique furniture, dusty stone sculptures.

"From the South Pacific," Nima said, pointing to a large, crumbling block that resembled a human head.

They went up a flight of wooden stairs that played a symphony of creaks, then reached a doorway and Nima stood aside. "The room," he announced.

Josh stepped inside and surveyed the space. Like the rest of the house, it was dark and musty. Along one wall stood a huge mahogany writing desk. In front of it was a magician's throne with a back that arched into a narrow spine six feet high. In each corner sat a high heel-shaped chair covered with leopard-skin velvet. Everything was coated in dust. Josh ran a finger across the table and a clean line appeared.

He stood in the middle of the room. It was certainly distant from his vision of LA life. He'd imagined minimalist living; wooden floors, white leather couches, a room flooded with light, one wall a giant window, looking out onto a deck with a shimmering turquoise swimming pool that seemed to disappear over the edge. This was different. This felt like a dusty old props cupboard in a disused theater.

"So?" Nima said.

It wasn't ideal, but Josh was desperate. And something told him that however weird it felt, somehow there was a place for him here. Somehow, he could make it home.

"I'll take it," he said.

"Excellent," said Nima. "There'll be some paperwork, of course. Just some formalities."

He passed back out of the house and Josh followed him. Back in the garden, Nima offered Josh some cherries and they stood munching quietly, content that they had reached an agreement.

As Josh stood eating, he looked out across the garden. He looked through the foliage, out west towards the Pacific. Peering through the tree branches, he could just make out the ocean and the sun beyond. It was far away, but he could sense its light and its warm glow.

"Nima…" he said.

But when he turned around, Nima had disappeared. There was

just an empty spot in the middle of the garden.

Chapter 11

Over the coming days, Josh settled into his room. As he rearranged the furniture, the dust gradually disappeared and a new layer emerged. He threw a couple of rugs down onto the floor and finally unpacked his stuff. At last, he had a place he could call home.

But there was still one major thing missing. He had no way of getting about. Walking around the city, he felt like some primitive creature, a Neanderthal beamed into a future world. It was Los Angeles, everyone kept telling him; he would need a car. But he couldn't afford one. All he could afford was a bike. And anyway, that was what he was determined to use.

So, one afternoon, he headed down to Santa Monica to investigate. As soon as he stepped into the first bike shop, he knew he wouldn't be able to resist. He didn't need the enthusiastic staff with shiny, shaved legs and handle-bar mustaches to persuade him. Within twenty minutes, he emerged with a bike that he could only ever have dreamed of owning; dazzling sky-blue, carbon frame, slick aluminum gears–all light enough to lift with one finger. It would make an unfortunate dent in his bank balance, but it was a beautiful bike.

That afternoon, he went to the beach front for a test ride. It was slick and smooth, and he purred with satisfaction as he cruised the streets. Gliding up and down the Venice boardwalk, he gazed out across the beach. He looked at all the classic LA things that he had grown up seeing on TV, amazed that they were actually real. There really were palm trees that rose high into the air, swaying gently against the vast, blue sky. There really were people in thongs, pumping iron on Muscle Beach. People really did use skateboards as a viable method of transportation. And there really were little blue huts along the beach front with orange floats hanging outside them. As he gazed out across the beach, he imagined himself in *Baywatch*, tearing off his T-shirt, grabbing an orange float, sprinting across the sand with his pectoral muscles flopping up and down, and diving into the sea.

He spent the rest of the day cruising the neighborhoods south of Santa Monica. Then, in the evening, he headed home. By the time he got back to the house, the sun was beginning to set. He went down into the garden, climbed into the hammock that Nima usually lay in, and immediately went *flop*. His whole body ached. It was a deep ache that came from using muscles that hadn't been exercised in years and sitting in positions he had never sat in. His body slumped in the netting and the hammock swung gently from side to side as it adjusted to his weight.

He lay there, looking up into the trees. Only gradually did he become aware of Nima. He was on the other side of the garden, spooning something into a little wooden box attached to a tree trunk.

"What are you doing?" Josh said.

"Feeding the birds," replied Nima.

He dipped his spoon into the bowl in his hand and put it gently into the wooden box. "The humming birds. They need feeding at this time. Caramelized sugar and water. Together, they make nectar." He dipped his spoon in again, then fed it back into the wooden box, like putting food into the mouth of a baby. He continued until the bowl was empty. Then he closed the door on the box, turned, and walked back into the main part of the garden.

"Good day?" Josh said.

"Yes, thanks. Just gardening. And some yoga. You?"

"I bought a bike and did some more exploring. Around Santa Monica, then down to Venice. I'm exhausted. Feel like I've been riding a horse, not a bike."

"Venice," Nima said. "I used to live around there. You know, it's probably a nicer place to live than Venice in Italy nowadays. At least there are fewer tourists."

"It's named after Venice in Italy?"

"Sure. Some guy back in the 19th century. He tried to recreate it, here on the West Coast."

Nima smiled and put the bowl down on the table. Then he sat down in one of the deck chairs and looked out through the trees.

"The Old World, transferred to the New," he said. "Like us."

"What do you mean?" Josh said.

"It's the same as us Iranians. From the Old World, to the New."

Josh had been wondering where Nima was from, but felt nosy to ask. "Where in Iran did you grow up Nima?"

"You know the Zagros Mountains?"

"No."

"They're along the western side. That's where I grew up. A village in the foothills of Mount Oshturan."

Josh lay in the hammock and waited. He sensed Nima wanted to continue.

"It was wonderful," Nima said. "Simple, but wonderful."

"Why?"

"Our village was tiny. Just a piece of land in the middle of the mountains. Remote. It felt like we were shut off from the rest of the world. And, in the winter, we got several feet of snow. Then we really *were* cut off."

He turned to face Josh.

"But in summer, it was different. It was so hot that we dug steps down into the earth and lived in underground chambers. And we were on the migration route. The herdsmen passed by our village. We heard the bells on their goats echoing up through the valley."

Josh lay in the hammock and looked up through the branches of the trees. There was no doubt that Nima's description did make it sound seductive.

"We used to get water from the *qanats*," Nima said. "You know about the *qanats*?"

"No."

"Water channels. Running underground to bring melting snow down from the mountains. They run across the whole of Iran, like veins. We called the water from the *qanats* liquid light. We grew mulberries, pomegranates, and walnuts. Imagine Hawaii, but in the middle of the desert."

Josh lay in the hammock, savoring the vision.

"And we had animals. Goats and sheep. The kebab we made from those sheep was the tastiest kebab I've ever had in my life."

Josh felt his mouth begin to water.

"You know," he said. "It was a simple life. But at the same time, there was an order to it. A rhythm. How we did things. Everything fitted."

Josh lay in the hammock, still staring up through the trees. "What about America?" he said, after a while, turning his head to look at Nima through the netting. "What did you think about America?"

"America? Back then, we didn't know about it. I mean, we knew about it, but it was distant. I remember my mother saying, *don't worry about America–too far to visit, too far to trade with, too far to invade us*. That was our view of it."

Josh continued looking through the hammock at Nima. He was gazing away across the garden. "On one level," he said, "it was wonderful. We were happy. But on another level, I don't know. Somehow…" his sentence fizzled out.

"What?"

Nima turned to face him. "It felt like some kind of change was coming."

They fell into silence for a moment. Josh looked at him.

"What kind of change?"

"I don't know."

"Something bad?"

"No, not bad. But not good. Either way," he said, looking up at Josh, "it was there. We could feel it coming."

Chapter 12

Josh spent the next few days in a pleasant routine. Cycling around the city, he gradually got used to the lay of the land. Sometimes he went down to the beach, and other times up to the Santa Monica Hills. He would gaze out over the city, breathing in the cool, breezy air. Back at the house, he would sit with Nima. While Nima tended the garden, he would teach Josh words for the birds and the plants in Persian.

One Saturday morning, Josh had gotten up late. After making himself breakfast, he came downstairs to find Nima chatting to a friend. They had been drinking coffee and were sat at a table in the middle of the garden, birds twittering around them.

"Ah," he said, "and this is Josh, my new housemate."

Nima's friend stood up and extended his hand to greet him. "Pouya," he said.

Pouya–sporting a long mullet hairstyle, earrings, ripped jeans, and a shell suit top–looked like he'd stepped out of an '80s music video. He smiled at Josh and they shook hands. Nima pulled up a chair for Josh to sit on and he joined them at the table.

"So how's life here?" Pouya said. "Like the interior décor? Wacky, right?"

"It's unusual," Josh said.

"Hey," Nima said. "Josh even knows a bit of Persian."

"Yeah?"

"Nima's been teaching me garden words."

"Tell us some."

"Well, *benafshe* is a violet. *Shokufeh* is blossom."

"And *laleh*... has he taught you that one?"

"Yes. That's a... tulip."

"Great," Pouya said, laughing heartily. He paused, thinking. "Hey Josh, what are you doing this evening?"

"I'm meant to be job-hunting..."

"How would you like to come on TV and do an interview?"

"Er–" Josh had just taken a mouthful of breakfast cereal so he couldn't answer properly.

"I host a show. Out and about in LA, what's happening in showbiz, pop culture... I'm thinking we could do a little feature on you. As a newcomer to LA, from the East Coast, and that you speak Persian."

"I don't actually speak Persian."

"No, come on, you'd be great."

"OK. But I really don't know any Persian."

"Yes you do. I heard you. I've never met a foreigner who spoke Persian before. I mean, never."

"But that's the only thing..."

"...even if it's only a few words. Come on. You'll be great..."

"Go on," Nima chipped in. "You'll be great. I know it."

"...I really don't think..."

"You're being modest," Pouya said. "It'll be fun. Look, I gotta dash right now. But I'll be back here at four. Pick you up then?"

Josh was about to protest, but he'd just taken another mouthful of cereal. He tried to shake his head to indicate *no*, but it was too late.

Pouya smiled. "Great," he said, draining his coffee and standing up. "I'll see you guys later."

***

At four that afternoon, Pouya returned and they set off.

They passed through the winding streets of Brentwood then joined the 405 and drove north. The sun was dazzling and, as they climbed the hill, Josh could feel the *whump, whump* of the gaps in the asphalt under the car. Over the crest, they began to descend the other side. Ahead of them lay a vast area of land, so flat it looked like it had been leveled by a gigantic bomb, like the aftermath of nuclear annihilation.

"What's that?" Josh said.

"The San Fernando Valley," Pouya said, looking into his rearview mirror while changing lanes.

They cruised down the other side and began to cross the valley. After a short distance, they turned off the freeway, drove along some back streets, and pulled up at an office block. Pouya

54

parked the car while Josh waited for him on the sidewalk. Looking around, he saw massive sun-parched mountains, straight roads in every direction, and clusters of signs thinning into the distance.

They crossed the road and entered the building together. Getting out of the elevator on the fourth floor, they passed a series of doors to edit suites and studios. A girl with a clipboard hurried past them, then two technicians carrying lighting equipment. At the end of the corridor, they passed another room, from which came tinny pop music, then they emerged into a lobby area with large, black leather couches. Pouya filled two plastic cups from a water cooler. He handed one to Josh and they sat down.

"So, what'll happen is, the show will begin, I'll do a short introduction, I'll ask you some questions–simple things: how you're finding life here after the East Coast, why you speak Persian, what you're doing in LA… by the way," he said, taking a gulp of water, "what *are* you doing in LA?"

"Oh, you know, nothing much, just…" His sentence trailed off.

"Not sure?" Pouya said. "Don't worry, none of us are." He finished his water, threw his cup in the bin and stood up. "Right, I've gotta go get prepped. Back soon."

Josh remained on the couch. He ran through all the words that Nima had taught him, just in case Pouya asked him to perform in the interview.

A few moments later, Pouya reappeared.

"Right," he said. "Time to rock and roll."

They got up and Josh followed Pouya back down the corridor into the studio. Inside it was dim, with technicians standing around, ghoulish specters in the dark. Josh picked his way through the clutter, carefully stepping over cables. Arriving on the set–a heavily lit, bright-blue expanse–his eyes squinted under the dazzling lamps. There was a tall metal table and two stools either side. Pouya sat down on one and Josh sat down on the other. He tried to adjust his eyes to the lights while Pouya looked at some papers on his clipboard.

A moment later, a woman appeared. She hurried around the

studio making last minute checks and giving orders. In one corner, a screen showed what was currently on air–a commercial of some kind. *Are you interested in a career with the CIA? Do you want to devote yourself to protecting the American homeland? If so, there are opportunities for native Persian speakers. Call 323 'homeland'.*

Then the ads ended. The sound on the monitor went off. The woman took up a position behind the camera and started a countdown. She spoke the numbers out loud at first, then mouthed the final few. As she reached zero, Pouya looked up from his clipboard, wiggled like a bird ruffling its feathers, and looked with a bright face and wide eyes towards the camera.

"*Saallaamm*," he said. "Welcome to *Sedaye Shoma,* live from the studios of *Pasargadae Entertainment* in Los Angeles. I'm your host, Pouya Behzadi. And we have a *fantastic* lineup for you today."

Josh sat in his chair, trying not to fidget, smiling weakly and wondering whether the camera was on him yet.

"In tonight's show, we have an interview with the hottest new Persian pop sensation in LA, news of the latest films from the Iranian diaspora, and, later, we're going to be talking about the Iranian entries at this year's *Oscars*. But, before all that, I'd like to welcome a very special guest."

Josh sensed that attention was now on him. He sat up in his chair and smiled towards the camera.

"So, without further ado, let me introduce you to… Josh!"

Josh continued smiling towards the camera. Pouya turned to face him.

"So, Josh," he said, "would you like to introduce yourself?"

Josh opened his mouth to speak. Suddenly it felt very dry.

"Salaam," he said.

"Salaam, Josh," Pouya said. "And welcome to the show."

Josh smiled again, weakly.

"Josh is a transplant from the East Coast. Just recently arrived in LA. So, Josh, I've got to ask you first up. How are you finding life here?"

"It's great…"

"Adjusting OK?"

"Yeah, fine."

"Not finding it a cultural wasteland? We know what you snooty East-coasters say about us over there."

"No, I kind of like it…"

"He says that now," Pouya said, turning to the camera. "Ask him in a year…"

He turned back to face Josh. "So, anyway, you were on the East Coast, and now you're in LA. What brought you here?"

"I graduated this summer, and moved to LA after that."

"Right, fair enough. Now then," he turned back to the camera. "There's a particular reason I invited Josh on the show today. Josh is a very gifted person. Josh, please reveal your special talent."

"Well…"

"Don't be shy…"

"I guess, all it is…"

"Come on now…"

"I speak Persian. Some Persian."

"Super," Pouya said, delighted. He turned back to face the camera. "So, let's have an example."

"Well, blossom is *shokufeh*…"

"Lovely…"

"… violet is *benafshe*…"

"Marvelous…"

"And *laleh* means… *laleh* is a tulip."

There was a moment's silence as Pouya looked transfixed, then he burst into applause.

"Bravo. Bravo. There we go. What an extraordinary thing! Well done, well done. Lovely accent. Central Iran, *Yazdi*, if I had to place it. So, Josh, before we wrap up… here you are on Persian TV… is there anything you'd like to say?"

"No, not really…"

"Like, a message to our viewers…?"

"Er–"

"Anything you like…"

"I can't really think of anything…"

"Absolutely sure?"

"Nothing springs to mind…"

"Sure you don't want," Pouya said, turning back to the camera, "to send a message that if there are any Persian girls out there who would like to go out on a date, you should give us a call right now? I mean, how often do you find a nice American fella who speaks Persian, right?"

Josh had already been blushing during the interview, but now he felt his cheeks burn red like a fire bursting into life. He tried to say something but his throat had dried up like a parched river bed.

"I think," Pouya continued, "he's saying that's correct. So, to any young women out there who like the idea of Persian-speaking American boyfriend, call into the studio right now–I'll put you straight onto Josh!"

"Well Josh," Pouya said, turning back to face him and planting his hand on Josh's back, "it's been an absolute pleasure having you on the show. No doubt you'll be deluged with offers straight after we go off-air."

"And so, viewers," he said, standing up from his chair, "onto our first feature…"

The camera panned across to Pouya. Josh remained in his chair, trying to suppress the burning sensation in his cheeks. He felt his back begin to clog with sweat. Then, a technician appeared, took his arm, and led him off set. They picked their way through the studio and emerged into the corridor outside.

In the lobby area, he poured himself a cup of water from the cooler and drank it slowly. *Jesus*, he thought. He couldn't believe Pouya had said that. It must have made him look totally ridiculous. I mean, that had gone out to the whole city, the whole country, the whole… he realized he wasn't even sure where this channel broadcast. But anyone who'd seen it would think he was a total *idiot*. He flopped down on the couch, suddenly resentful that he'd been persuaded to come and do the show in the first place.

He sat slumped on the couch like a zombie, staring ahead. He looked up at a monitor above him. They were now on more ads. A man was talking directly into the camera holding a jar and, below him, flashed the caption: *Authentic Iranian soil, fresh from the Alborz Mountains. $20 a jar.*

Josh sat in the couch, paralyzed with fury. He was so absorbed in his rage that he barely saw the man passing slowly through the lobby. Only at the last moment did he notice him. He was older than everyone else in the studio; his white linen suit made him look like a gentle retiree, the lapels of his jacket flapping lazily around him like he had just stepped off a yacht. Beneath his open-neck shirt, his skin was glazed like a basted turkey and the scent of his cologne was strong. He was just about to pass when he stopped and looked down at Josh sitting on the couch.

"Ah," he said.

Josh looked up.

"I saw you. The American who speaks Persian."

"I'm sorry about that…"

"No, it was very good," he said. There was a pause. "Come with me," he said, motioning to Josh to follow. "You can wait in here."

Josh got up and they walked together down the corridor to his office.

"Take a seat," he said, pointing to a chair in front of the table.

Josh sat down and looked around the room. There were more black leather couches and a huge glass table stood in the middle. TV screens lined the walls, covering the room like a sports bar. Ads were still playing: *Hair removal services… no growth too big or too small. Call us now for a quote.*

The man walked round to the other side of the table and sat down in a large, black leather swivel chair. He picked up two remote controls and, holding one in each hand, spun round to face one of the screens. He leaned back and pointed a remote to change the channel.

"I heard your interview," he said, looking at the TV screen.

"It wasn't quite–"

"You speak Persian very well."

"Hardly…"

"No, it's good. And with a slight *Esfahani* accent."

"Pouya said it was…"

"I liked that," he said. "I liked it." He held out his hand. "I'm Mr. Behzadi."

"Josh."

They shook hands and Mr. Behzadi resumed flicking through the channels. Suddenly, there was a sharp knock at the door. The head of a young man appeared, leaning into the room. His black hair was parted neatly at the side and he was agitated and breathless, his forehead gleaming with sweat.

"Mr. Behzadi, I'm so sorry to interrupt," he said, sweeping the mop of hair back from over his face.

"What's the trouble?"

"Problems with *Channel Two* again..."

"What now?"

"They're accusing you of defection..."

"Why?"

"You used the wrong flag in the news broadcast yesterday."

"We used the flag we always use..."

"Yes, but they say that's the old flag..."

Mr. Behzadi sighed. "OK. Is that all?"

"No. They've also started that rumor about you again."

"Which rumor?"

"That you're taking money from the Islamic Republic. They had it halfway through the early evening news."

Mr. Behzadi sat in his chair calmly, the remote controls flopped lazily at his side. "This evening's news?"

"Yes."

"Presented by Dariyush Farzan?"

"That's right."

He sat quietly, thinking. The young man at the door hung on expectantly. There was a long pause, then Mr. Behzadi turned to face him.

"Tell the news team to revise their running order for tonight. Tell them to prepare a piece about *Channel Two* taking money from the Islamic Republic for their new studio. Put it at the top of tonight's headlines."

The man nodded vigorously. "No problem. I'll tell them right away." He turned to leave.

"And, also, Shahryar...?"

"Yes?"

"Call *Channel Two*. Tell them we have photographic evidence of their director and president embezzling corporation funds at a casino in Vegas over Christmas."

"Absolutely. Is that all?"

"That's all."

The young man ducked out of the room. Mr. Behzadi turned around slowly in his chair to face Josh. He sighed. "You know, there are twenty-odd Iranian TV stations here in LA. But, *be khoda*, sometimes it feels like we spend more time attacking each other than the government in Iran."

Mr. Behzadi put the remotes down on the table, got up, and walked across to the window. He stood with his hands in his pockets, looking out across the Valley.

"I remember when I first came to this city." He waved his hand across the window. "None of this was here. No Iranians. No TV stations. And now, look. The airwaves are full of us. We've taken over. Here we are, in the city of Britney Spears, and everyone's listening to Persian pop!"

Josh sat in his chair, half listening. He was still quietly fuming about the interview.

Mr. Behzadi turned around to face him from the window. "You know, sometimes I still can't believe we're here at all."

Josh stopped sulking and looked up. "But... why are you here?"

"Why? Because of the Revolution. You know about the Revolution, surely?"

"No."

"You don't know...?" He sighed and trailed off.

"What was the Revolution?"

"Well," he said. "Where should I begin?" He turned back to face the window. "I suppose from when I moved to Tehran. It was the autumn of 1977. I'd gone there to study."

"Things were peaceful then. Or at least, they seemed peaceful. The regime looked stable. I remember when Carter came for his New Year visit. Do you know what he said?"

Josh shook his head.

"Iran is an island of stability in a sea of uncertainty." He smiled to himself again and fell back into silence. He stood looking out the window for a few moments before continuing.

"Then something changed," he said. "I'm not sure when,

exactly. Maybe early 1978. There was a particular day. The government published an article on Khomeini. Said he wasn't a proper Muslim or something. On that day, something changed.

"There were protests. Big protests. The government didn't know what to do. When they put them down, people got angrier. And, when they didn't, they got more confident. It was a catch-22.

"Well, the protests got bigger. By the autumn of 1978, they were really big. Hundreds of thousands of people. And it wasn't just the Islamists. Everybody. Everyone was out on the streets." He paused. "But still," he said, turning to face Josh, "the funny thing was, even at that time, people thought it would blow over. People thought the regime would hold."

He stood and shook his head, as if he couldn't quite believe it to be true.

"And when did things change?" Josh said. "When did people realize the government would fall?"

"I think," he said, speaking slowly now, "I think that happened in late 1978. There was a moment. I don't know when it was *exactly*, but there was definitely a moment. People realized. They saw there was no going back. And they were right. A few weeks later, the Shah left the country. That was the end."

Mr. Behzadi walked from the window back to his chair and sat down. As he sat at the table, Josh could see, behind his eyes, the events being replayed in his head.

"We should have seen it coming. Even now, I say to myself, how did we not see it coming?"

He sat at his desk, lost in thought. Josh sat thinking, still cursing Pouya for what he had said, but now also thinking about what Mr. Behzadi had been telling him.

They were both sitting silently when another knock came from the door. This time, Pouya appeared in the doorway. He was holding a small piece of paper, dangling it in front of him.

"Josh! So sorry. Show went on longer than expected. Listen, we've got to go. I'm heading back to the Westside. I can drop you home. And hey," he said, holding aloft the piece of paper, "great news. I think I've found a Persian girlfriend for you."

Chapter 13

The following day, Josh sat in his room, holding the piece of paper. It was just a small scrap. All it had written on it was the name *Noushin* and a phone number. He read it over a few times, then picked up his mobile, and punched in the numbers. He held the handset to his ear, listening to the ringtones. One ring… two rings… then there was a pause.

"Hello?" came a voice.

"Hi, is that Noushin?"

"Speaking. Who's this?"

"It's Josh."

"Josh…"

"From the TV studio. Pouya gave me your number–"

"Oh! *Josh*. Yes. So nice to hear from you. Pouya told me *all* about you."

"Right. Well, I was calling to see if, you know, you wanted to–"

"To meet up? Oh, that's great, Josh. I'd love to. When could it be?"

"I don't know. We could–"

"Well, I don't know about you, but I'm free… oh, I'm free tonight actually."

"OK, well, let's do tonight."

"Great. Where shall we meet?"

"Well, I'm kind of new in town…"

"How about *Angelo's* on Sunset? Do you know it?"

"No."

"Doesn't matter. You'll like it. See you there at, say, eight?"

"Fine."

"And let's say, PST."

"PST?"

"Persian Standard Time. You know, eight, *give or take*."

"I see. Got it. Well, see you later."

"Wonderful! See you there. Mwah."

And the line went dead.

Josh put the phone down. Well, that had been remarkably

easy, he thought. For a moment, he thought perhaps *too* easy. But, no, why be negative? He was going out on a date and that could only be good news.

Down in the garden, Nima was lying in his hammock, swinging gently, cracking open pistachio nuts and dropping the shells into a bowl beneath.

"How are things?"

"Quite good, actually. You know when I went to the TV studio…"

"Yes?"

"Pouya gave me someone's number. And we're going out on a date tonight."

"Well done," he said. "Who is she?"

"She's called Noushin."

Nima just smiled. "Good luck."

***

Josh spent the rest of the day preparing for the date. Nima had a dusty, old iron–a sort of antique specimen–which he ran over his clothes. He looked up *Angelo's* on the map. For a moment, he thought about cycling. But after checking the distance, he realized it was just a little too far. And anyway, he didn't want to arrive soaked through with sweat. There was only one option. He would have to take the bus.

Noushin had said eight, *give or take*. Josh assumed that meant give. But there was always a chance it could mean take. In the past, he had gone wrong on first dates by arriving late. This time, he was taking no risks. He got an early bus and waited on the sidewalk. Darkness was falling and he stood in the warm haze of the evening, watching the glow of the neon slowly emerge as the traffic crawled along Sunset Boulevard.

Forty minutes later, at nearly half past eight, he heard a screeching sound behind him. He turned round and saw a long, silver *Mercedes* jerking unsteadily along the street. It reached a sudden halt and reversed into a small parking spot. Then the engine went dead and a woman climbed out. She reached back

64

into the car to grab one, two, *three* purses, slammed the door, and strode across the street, or rather, strode as fast as her slender high heels would allow. She wore a tight pair of navy-blue jeans that tapered down from her waist to slender calves and, at the bottom, seemed to taper away into nothing. On top, she was wearing a tight blouse and a small navy jacket. She wasn't plump, but there was something about her clothes that made her *seem* plump, as if she had had to hold her breath for a moment to do the zip all the way. Her dark hair rose up from her head in a wavy bouffant as if she had just emerged from a wind tunnel. As she crossed the road, she beamed a broad smile that revealed unnaturally white teeth.

"God!" she said, frizzing her hair with her hands as if she had just stepped out of the shower and were using an invisible towel. "Traffic *nightmare*. Some kind of accident on the 405. Then..." she kissed the air around his ears "... a total parking *fiasco*." She stood back to look at Josh. "Where did you put yours?"

"I came by bus."

Noushin stood with a blank expression, waiting for more.

"The bus," Josh said. "I don't have a car."

Her face dropped for a moment. "You don't...? Oh, but you've only just arrived in LA, right?"

"Right."

"Well. That explains..." She made some more small adjustments to her hair. Then she patted Josh on the arm. "Come on, let's go."

She led the way, tottering along the sidewalk, and Josh trailed behind. At the restaurant, they pushed through the glass doors. Inside, a handsome, suited man stood at a kiosk greeting people. The subdued lighting submerged the whole place in shadow. Candles on the tables cast flickering lights on the diners. Josh couldn't see what they looked like but, in the gloom, they all appeared incredibly glamorous.

Like a honing missile, Noushin charted a course straight to the bar. As she arrived, she paused, then turned around. She mouthed the words *"you hungry?"* while rubbing her stomach, and changed direction towards the dining area. Josh was about to suggest that a drink would probably be enough but, before he could intervene, Noushin had found a table, put her bags down, and pulled out a seat. She draped her jacket over the back.

Josh joined her, took off his jacket, hung it over the chair, and sat down opposite. The table looked out over Sunset Boulevard, the traffic jammed bumper-to-bumper along the street. As he sat down, he felt the unpleasant feeling that, already, the evening was starting to go wrong.

"All looks very good," Noushin said, head buried in the menu. It was a large, white, card menu with silver, embossed lettering–each item listed without the dollar sign, as if to soften the blow, or make it seem like it had nothing to do with money.

"So, Josh," Noushin said, looking up from the menu. "Tell me… all… about… *you.*"

"Well, I was born in New Jersey. Then when–"

Noushin thrust her hand forward and grabbed his arm. "Oh! I just *love* your accent." She wagged her head slowly from side to side and looked at him intently. "It's so… *sexy.*"

There was a pause. Josh waited, expecting her to laugh it off as a joke, but she continued to shake her head and look at him wistfully. She looked at him for a moment more, then took her hand off his arm and nodded as if signaling him to continue speaking.

"As I was saying… I grew up in New Jersey then I went to college in Massachusetts. Not sure why I went there, perhaps I should have…"

He glanced at Noushin and noticed her eyes had strayed back to the menu. He stopped what he was saying, expecting her to notice, but she didn't. So, he picked up his menu, and started browsing the offerings. A moment later, a waiter appeared beside them. His white shirt and black waist coat, with trimmed, black, goatee beard, made him look like a magician.

"Evening, sir, madam. I'm Vincent. I'll be your server tonight. Have you decided what you'd like to drink?"

Noushin picked up the wine list and scanned it for a moment. She puckered her lips as if applying serious thought to the matter.

"I'll have…" she pointed with her index finger, "the *Chablis.*"

"Very good. And you, sir?" he said, turning to Josh.

"Just water for me, thanks."

"Still or sparkling?"

"Tap water is fine," he said quietly.

"I'm sorry?"

"*Tap* water is fine."

"Very good. And to eat? Or would you like more time?"

"No, I think we're ready," Noushin said. "I'll have..." she scrolled down the menu with her finger, lips pursed, eyes concentrating rigorously, "the lobster."

"Very good. And you, sir?"

"I'll just have the..." Josh searched frantically for something that might keep the final check under three figures, "a salad..."

"Any particular type of salad?"

"Just a... vegetarian salad."

"And, anything to go with that?"

"No, that's all, thanks."

"Excellent." Vincent plucked the menus out of their hands and disappeared into the maze of low-slung tables.

Noushin settled in her chair and, for the first time, really looked at Josh. She ran her eyes over him, like a vet inspecting an animal. She carefully noted his hair and clothes, finishing off with his phone and wallet on the table. Finally, she made a '*humph*' noise, like she was satisfied, although Josh felt unsure whether this was satisfaction with him, or just satisfaction that the inspection was complete.

"So, Josh, you're from New Jersey..."

"That's right."

"And you studied at...?"

"Harvard."

Her eyebrows went up with satisfied surprise.

"What was your major?"

"Liberal arts."

"Right..."

"Mainly art history..."

"Oh. That's nice. I love art. Just..." she held her hands out in front of her like she was trying to grasp something elusive but profound that hovered in the air, "... *love* it." He thought she was going to add something, but she didn't. "So," she said, "what are you going to do with that?"

"Not sure, really. I mean, I might become a journalist. Or a writer…"

"A writer?"

"Yes."

"You mean, you're going to write *books*?"

"Yes."

There was a pause. Noushin mulled something over in her head. "Do writers earn much?"

"Some do."

"I suppose so. I mean, *Fifty Shades*… whoever wrote that must be doing well. Or *Harry Potter*." She fell into silence for a moment. "Anyway," she said, brushing this topic aside. "Right now you are…?"

"I just arrived in California, so I'm looking for a job."

"So you're unemployed?"

"Yes."

"*Right*," she said, with an expression like she'd trodden in something weird but wasn't yet sure what it was.

At that moment, Vincent arrived with the drinks.

"*Chablis* and… water."

"And some bread?" said Noushin, turning to look at him.

"With you in a moment."

Noushin picked up her glass and took a sip while turning her head away to look out the window. Josh picked up his glass and took a sip of water. They sat in silence. After a moment, Vincent returned with a basket of bread. He put it on the table and Noushin peered at it, then plucked out a large piece, rolled it up, and popped it in her mouth.

"So," she said, bread in both cheeks, "have you ever been on a date with a Persian girl before?"

"I thought you were Iranian."

"Persian," she said, rolling up another bit of bread and smoothing it over with butter.

"I thought Persian was a language…"

"Maybe in some places. But not in LA. I mean, in New York, or London, you're Iranian. But in LA, you're Persian."

"Right…"

"It's like our race. Everyone here has a race. You're either black, or white, or Hispanic, or Asian. Well, we're Persian."

Josh was trying to think of something else to say when Vincent arrived with the food. He carried the plates on his arm and stood over them at the table.

"Lobster," he said, easing a groaning platter onto the table. He turned to Josh. "And the salad." He put a tiny bowl down in front of him. Noushin cast a sympathetic look in his direction, then rolled up her sleeves and maneuvered herself into position. Josh took a fork and began picking through his salad leaves.

"Bon appétit!" she said, dismantling her lobster. She looked at it with focused concentration, like a brain surgeon performing an operation.

"So," Josh said, chewing his first mouthful of lettuce. "How many Persians are there in LA?"

"Some people say half a million." She kept her eyes firmly on the task in front of her. "Others say two million." She put a piece of discarded shell on a side dish. "Really, nobody knows."

"How come?"

"Well..." she stopped and picked up a piece of lobster shell and cracked it in her teeth. The meat fell out onto her plate. She scooped it up and popped it in her mouth. "The problem is... the census. In the census, there's no category for Persians. You're either white, or Middle Eastern. As you know, Persians are *not* Middle Eastern. So, we just say we're white. It's easier that way."

"So, technically, you're white..."

"Yeah. Funny, isn't it? I think there's a term for it. Whitewashed, or something."

Noushin bit into another piece of lobster leg. Josh heard a crunch and wondered whether it was the lobster or her teeth. She paused to pick another bit of shell out from her mouth.

"You know," she said, fingers rummaging between her teeth, "sometimes it's difficult being Persian. I mean, we get treated weird. Sometimes people think we're terrorists because we're from Iran. But, actually, there aren't *any* terrorists from Iran. And sometimes people think we're white. We're like the unknown, mystery people. It's kind of funny."

She fell into silence and continued eating. Josh resumed munching his salad. He glanced outside at the traffic on Sunset. It was moving quicker now and a succession of cars glided past the window. He sat and watched them go by, chewing on his food. They sat and ate in silence for a few minutes. It was just was beginning to get awkward when he remembered the conversation he'd had the previous day.

"Yesterday I was chatting to this guy..."

"Hhmm..." Noushin said, without looking up at him. By now her plate was piled high with bits of lobster shell.

"... and he was telling me about the Revolution."

Noushin groaned. "Oh. The *Revolution.*"

Josh raised his eyebrows.

"The older generation," she said. "It's all they talk about." She wiped her mouth. "So, what was he saying?"

"I can't remember. How... it was really big..."

"Yes..."

"And how no one saw it coming..."

"Well, that's true." She swallowed another mouthful of lobster and dabbed her chin with her napkin.

"It's funny. I mean, you would have thought something that big, someone would have seen it coming..."

"Yeah, well, no one did," Noushin replied.

Josh went quiet. He sensed Noushin wanted to change the subject.

"... I guess," he wondered aloud, "... it must have been weird coming to California..."

"Well," she said, "I wasn't actually around then. I mean, I was born here, *after* the Revolution."

"But your parents must remember..."

Noushin placed her knife and fork down, wiped her mouth a final time, scrunched up her napkin, and put it on her plate.

"I don't really know," she said. She paused, looking outside. "But I don't think it was too weird. The main thing they always talk about is the parties."

"Parties?"

"People left Iran. But they didn't think it was forever. They thought it was short term. They thought they were on vacation."

"Right…"

"The Revolution happened in January. It was the middle of winter. Everyone was leaving. So where did they go? Not New York. It was freezing. They came to LA. They wanted sunshine."

"And they partied?"

"Yes. They had a good time. They thought they were on holiday."

"OK." There was a moment's silence. "And then what happened?"

"Well, they partied for a few months, then they realized they could be here for a while. They started to think about actually *living* here."

"And what was that like?"

"Probably pretty strange at first. I mean, LA back in the '70s was a weird place. Fluorescent pink leggings. Baggy sweatshirts. Neon leg warmers. That stuff had never made it to Iran."

Josh took a sip of his drink.

"And it was *backward.* In the '70s, you couldn't get proper coffee in LA. It was a Persian guy who opened the first espresso joint in Westwood. And there weren't things like street dining. Then the Persians arrived and everyone was eating on the streets. It was just a totally different place." She paused, thinking. "But at the same time…" she said, then her sentence trailed off.

"What?"

"At the same time," she spoke slowly, picking her words, "… in a funny way, some people felt LA was… *familiar.*"

"What do you mean?"

She leaned forward, as if finally warming to the conversation. "Tehran and LA are on opposite sides of the earth. Drill a hole from here and eventually you'll reach Tehran. But at the same time… they actually have quite a lot in common."

"Like?"

"Let's see… first, the mountains. Where's Tehran? Just under the Alborz Mountains. And LA? Right in the middle of the Santa Monicas. Look at Downtown on a winter day and I swear it looks just like Tehran."

"OK. What else?"

"The desert."

"The desert?"

"Yes. Drive two hours out of LA and you're in the Mojave Desert. It's pretty much identical to the desert around Tehran."

"OK… mountains, desert. Anything else?"

"Well, then there's the traffic."

"How do you mean?"

"The only place with jams as big as Tehran is LA. You've seen the traffic on the 405. I mean, those jams are practically visible from *space*."

"So, mountains, desert, traffic…"

"And what comes with traffic?"

"Pollution?"

"Exactly. LA's pollution isn't as bad as it was. But, back in the '80s, it was *seriously* bad."

"And Tehran…?"

"… has the worst pollution in the world. Literally. In summer, you have to wear a gas mask. You've a better chance surviving a nuclear apocalypse than Tehran in summer."

"So we've got mountains, desert, traffic and pollution…"

"Hang on. There's one more thing." She looked around, like a teacher trying to find a prop to demonstrate something. Then she had an idea. She put her hands down on either side of the table and gripped the edges, looking Josh firmly in the eyes. She started jiggling the table back and forth, gently at first, then with more energy, until the plates and glasses rattled around and nearby diners began to give them strange looks.

"Got it?" she said, over the noise.

"Earthquakes?!"

"*Exactly*," she said, relaxing her grip on the table and letting it rest back on the floor. "LA and Tehran sit on eruption zones, or whatever they're called. Each place is waiting for the big one. Any moment, either one of them could turn to *dust*."

They fell into silence then, all of a sudden, a figure appeared beside them.

"All done here?"

"Yes," Josh said. "We're done, thanks."

Vincent began to clear the table, placing their cutlery on the plates, scraping the bits of lobster shell onto a plate and piling the dishes up on his arm.

"Dessert?"

For a moment, Noushin's face lit up. Josh considered whether a strategic intervention would be worth the loss of face. But, fortunately, a moment later, she conceded defeat. "You know, I think I'm full."

"I think we just need the check," Josh said.

"Very good. With you in a flash."

"So," Noushin said, turning back to face him. "Maybe that's why LA and Tehran were sister cities. Back in the '70s, before the Revolution." She smiled. "I mean, don't get me wrong, I'm not saying people in LA actually think they're in Iran. But somehow, *subconsciously*, it must be familiar."

Vincent returned promptly with the check. As he slid the dish onto the table, Josh reached into his pocket for his wallet. He was already resigned to covering it. Actually, he didn't mind so much anymore.

"Don't worry," Noushin said. "This is on me."

Josh didn't know what to say. "Really?"

"It's fine. You barely ate anything anyway."

Vincent produced a card reader and Noushin punched in her numbers. When it was done, they got up and passed back through the restaurant, saying goodbye to the man at the kiosk and emerging out onto the Sunset sidewalk. It was fully dark now and the neon lights shone brightly along the street in a jumble of illuminated signs. The traffic was row upon row of red and white lights. The air was thick and warm.

Noushin turned to Josh. "Well, that was a really lovely evening. I had a good time."

"Me too."

She paused. "Hang on," she said, "how are you getting home?"

"I'll get the bus."

"How long does that take?"

"Not long. It goes straight along Sunset."

She looked at Josh, then looked along the street.

"Come on. I can't take you all the way. But I'll give you a ride to the bus stop."

Josh thought better than to turn down the offer. They crossed the road and got into the car. Noushin turned on the engine, pulled out into the street, and they set off along Sunset. They didn't say anything for a few minutes. After a while, Josh broke the silence.

"Well, Noushin… that was a really lovely evening."

"It was. Thank you."

They fell back into silence, Noushin with her eyes on the road, Josh pretending to look out the window.

"I really had a good time," he said.

"Me too. It was fun."

More silence. Noushin looked ahead at the traffic and Josh stared ahead, too.

"Yeah, I mean, it was nice. And, you know, I could imagine… maybe… that it might be nice to…"

Noushin was looking firmly ahead, as if she couldn't hear. Josh waited a moment for her to say something, but nothing came.

"I mean, what I was saying was… if you wanted… you know… if you wanted to do it again…"

Noushin continued to stare ahead.

"… to go for dinner… or a drink…"

"Oh," Noushin said suddenly. "There's the bus stop." She pulled the steering wheel violently to the left and the car U-turned onto the other side of the street. Then she swerved over towards the sidewalk and brought them to a sharp halt. There was silence as Josh caught his breath from the maneuver.

"So, here you are. I hope you don't have to wait too long."

"Thanks."

There was a pause.

"So," he said, "as I was saying just now…"

Josh heard Noushin take a sudden sharp breath of air. Then she sighed, reached forward to turn off the engine, and turned around in her seat.

"Look, Josh," she said, re-adjusting her gaze from the traffic to him. "I'm glad you had a nice time tonight. I enjoyed it, too."

Josh looked at her face, waiting for what was to come.

"But, I'm going to be blunt here. I don't think there's any point us meeting up again."

"Oh. OK. Well, I wasn't–"

"It's not because you're not a nice guy. I mean, you're clearly a really nice guy."

"Thanks…"

"I just don't see us… hitting it off."

"Well, that's fine… I didn't expect us to–"

"I mean, the issue of you not having a car is kind of important."

"Right. Fair enough."

"And the fact that you don't have a *job*…"

"Sure, sure… I can see that too…"

They fell into silence. Josh sat in the passenger seat without saying anything.

"Look," Noushin said, "I don't want to upset you. But, to be frank, I think the prospect of romance between us is as likely as… well, in Persian, we'd say as likely as a phoenix on the western horizon."

Josh was about to ask what exactly she meant by this, but then thought he'd probably got the gist. He looked down at the floor and wondered how long he should wait before opening the door to leave.

"Look," Noushin said, "you better go. You'll miss your bus."

He reached around for the handle and opened the door. He ducked his head as he got out, then stood with his hand on top of the car and stooped down.

"Thanks for the ride. It was nice to meet you."

"Take care, Josh. It was nice meeting you, too."

He closed the door with a thud, then the car pulled out, and drove off.

Josh turned around and walked over to the bus stop. He stood underneath the shelter and stared down the street, searching the oncoming lights for the distant shape of a bus. All that day, the weather had been warm. But now, for the first time, he shivered and felt a chill in the air. He thought of Yasmin. But even the thought of her warm skin against his did little to comfort him.

Chapter 14

A week later, Josh was sitting at home in the garden. The sun gently streamed through the foliage and water gurgled along the makeshift irrigation channels. He hadn't seen a single cloud since moving to LA. He'd been checking. Not a single one. That was two months now. Of course, on one level, it was lovely. But something about it also disturbed him. The relentless beating of the sun… was this even healthy?

As he sat in the garden, Nima moved between the trees feeding the humming birds.

"Nima," Josh said after a while. "Is everyone in LA Persian?"

Nima laughed. "Why do you ask?"

"It just seems every person I meet is from Iran."

"Well, you've just been hanging out in Iranian circles…"

"I guess…"

"What do you expect if you spend all your time in Tehrangeles?" He went back to watering the garden.

Josh had noticed a slight change in Nima's appearance recently. The baggy trousers had disappeared. Now, he left the house each morning wearing a brown suit and two-tone brown and white shoes, hair gelled neatly down, occasionally a fluffy, white handkerchief in his top pocket. He looked like a 1920s Chicago gangster.

"I've been meaning to ask, what's with the change of image Nima?"

"My new experiment."

"What's that?"

"Listen: *eh, mamma mia, mamma mia…*" He held his hand out with the fingers lightly pressed together. "*Spirito d'Italia.*"

"You're an Italian gangster…"

"Italian, yes. But not a gangster. *Look here, ve have 'ere de finest men's fashion. As you vill see, all,*" he screwed up his face for emphasis, "*authentic Italian.*"

"I'm lost. Explain."

"Friend of mine has a clothing store in Downtown. I'm renting it. Going to make it a men's fashion store."

"Right…"

"Nice idea, eh?"

"But, why Italian?"

"What are the options? Iranian? No one's heard of Iranian fashion. And anyway, this is America. It's the worst place on *earth* to be Iranian."

"But Italy's miles away. Why not something closer. Mexican?"

"Have you heard of Mexican fashion? And anyway, do you see me speaking Spanish? I'd get found out. No, Italian is the best. No one in LA speaks Italian. No one can figure me out."

He smoothed down the creases on his jacket. "Anyway," he said. "What about you?"

"Yeah, so so…"

"You look a bit down of late."

"Not down. Just… still settling in, I guess."

"California takes a while to get used to. It's a different lifestyle."

"I guess you're right."

"Actually, I've got a friend who might interest you. She runs workshops. Self-help… that sort of stuff. Not for people in a major fix. Just if you feel the need for some guidance. Especially about 'the California way'."

"OK…"

Nima handed him a leaflet. "Here's one of her fliers. Take a look."

Josh sat and read the flier aloud. "*Build a vibrational stair-step towards your own self-fulfillment.* Oh geez, Nima. I can't handle this stuff…"

"No, no, trust me. It'll be good."

"I see there's something on this evening."

"Well, go and check it out." And he went back to feeding his birds.

***

That evening, Josh set out on his bicycle. He cruised down the hilly streets of Brentwood, rattling over the cracks that riddled the streets like little veins, as if something were breaking up through the earth. Locking up his bicycle on Santa Monica Boulevard opposite the seafront, he found the venue–a swish glass-fronted restaurant over-looking the coastal road. He took a seat at the front and waited. A steady stream of people arrived, then the audience quietened down, and a woman stepped out from behind a curtain.

She wore a silky, black dress that came down to just above her knee, and black high heels. She had white skin and very dark eyes with dark eyelashes. She wore red lipstick and her hair was black and short, with a fringe that swept across her face. She walked across the stage stealthily, like a cat in high heels, and stood at the microphone at the front.

"Ladies, gentlemen," she said, surveying the audience. "Good evening. My name is Bita Taghavi. And I'd like to welcome you to this evening's event."

Conversation fell away and silence descended. The woman cast her eyes around the room. "I'm very happy you've made the effort to come this evening," she said. "I'm sure you'll all learn a lot from it."

She took the microphone from its stand, the cord in one hand, and began to walk around the stage.

"As you know, tonight's event is about relationships. And, by relationships, I mean your *romantic* relationships. Your relationships with your husbands, wives, boyfriends and girlfriends."

She came to the front of the stage. "So, first of all, I'd like to ask why you came tonight. Who came because they're experiencing problems with their marriage?"

People in the audience glanced around the room, but no one put their hands up.

"OK," she said. "Who came because they're having problems with a boyfriend or girlfriend?"

Again, there was silence.

"OK. Who came because they're having problems with their sex lives?"

Once again, no one put their hand up. Josh felt the silence in the room descend a little deeper.

The woman smiled. "You're all being very shy. But don't worry. I'm sure you'll loosen up."

"Well," she said, "I think we'll get things moving by talking a bit about *women*." She glanced down and lifted the microphone cable out the way of her feet.

"Now, you need to remember, there are fundamental differences between men and women. One is about how we communicate. Women like to talk, and talk, and talk. Even if what we're saying doesn't make sense, we find it reassuring just to talk."

Josh looked around and noticed some of the women in the audience scowling.

The woman continued. "Men, on the other hand, only talk when they have something specific to say." Josh looked around and noticed a number of men gently nodding their heads in agreement.

She walked over to a flip chart on the other side of the stage, picked up a pen, turned over the first sheet, and started drawing. A few moments later, she turned around.

"Right. Can anyone tell me what that is?"

There was silence from the audience. Finally, a voice came from the back. "A pineapple?"

The woman searched out the voice in the darkness. "That's right. It's a pineapple. Thank you. Can anyone tell me why I've drawn that?"

There was a pause. "Because that's what women are like?"

"Correct. Thank you very much. Women are like pineapples. Spiky on the outside, soft and sweet on the inside."

She turned back to the board and began drawing again. This time, she drew a jagged, zigzag line running diagonally from the bottom left to the top right.

"Now, can anyone tell me what *that* is?"

"A flight of stairs?" someone said.

"That's right," she said. "And what do flights of stairs do?"

"They go up and down?"

"Correct. They go up and down. Can anyone see the connection?"

Silence from the crowd.

"They go *up* and *down*. That's just like a man, isn't it?"

More silence.

"What I mean to say is, they have erections. *Right*?"

The silence was now all-encompassing, like all noise had been sucked out of the room. There was just the sound of fridges humming in the kitchen.

The woman smiled. "Well, I bet you never thought you'd hear a Persian woman say the word *erection* in public!"

An older man in a tweed jacket cleared his throat and brought his glass down on the table with a thump. Another woman leaned over to her deaf husband and whispered in his ear what had been said. And from somewhere in the room, Josh could hear the sound of a long, slow persistent *tut-tut*.

The talk went on for another forty-five minutes. At the end, the audience applauded and started to get up to leave. The woman left the stage, and went to sit behind a table with a display of books and DVDs. A small queue of people formed to ask questions and buy products. Josh hung back until they had all had a chance to speak, then he approached the woman.

"Excuse me, I enjoyed your talk."

She looked up at him. "Thanks," she said. "Slightly quiet audience tonight. But that happens. Did you find it helpful?"

"Yes."

"Hang on," she said, breaking off. "Will you excuse me a moment?"

Two younger women had arrived at the table and seemed keen to talk.

"Azita, Mahsa! Darlings!" There was a flurry of air kisses. "Listen, I want you to sign up for my new workshop. Discover your inner Amazonian woman."

"Do you think we can do it?"

"Sure you can. You'll be great. Here's the info. Starts next week. I'll see you there!"

Azita and Mahsa bounced off cheerfully, and the woman turned back to Josh.

"Would it be possible to ask you a couple of questions?" he said.

"I've got to go soon. But I can stick around for a few minutes. Take a seat and I'll come and join you."

Josh sat down at a nearby table. A short while later, the woman joined him, carrying a long, dark jacket and a black leather bag. She put them down on the next table then pulled up a chair and sat down.

"Hamid, joon, could you get me a small glass of wine?" She turned to Josh. "Would you like one?"

"I'm fine, thanks."

"Just one Hamid joon. Thank you."

"By the way," she said. "I'm Bita."

"Josh."

She held out her hand and they shook across the table.

"So," she said. "I'm curious. Why did you come along this evening?"

"My housemate suggested it. I recently moved here from the East Coast. He said I needed to adjust to Californian living."

"Right. But... it surprises me. I don't get many Americans along to these events. Most of my clientele are Persian."

"I wondered about that."

"Not everyone. But most." Her wine arrived. Hamid put it down on the table and she thanked him.

"You could say it's a little surprising," she said, taking a sip. "I mean, in Iranian culture, self-help, dating advice... it's not really our thing. But over here in LA? Well, that's a different story." She drank some more wine, then put it back on the table.

"Remember," she said, "Californian society is totally different from Iran. *Totally* different."

"How exactly?"

"Think about it. Iranian culture is conservative. We've got our particular ways of doing things."

"And California..."

"California?" she said, smiling. "In California, anything goes. It's the land of the wacky. World capital of the weird. People pride themselves on being bizarre. So, for Iranians, it's like taking someone totally sane and putting them in an asylum."

She took another sip before continuing. "You know how in Iran it's the men who run everything? Or at least, it's the men who *think* they run everything?"

Josh nodded.

"Well, over here, the women run the show. We've got more opportunities to get out of the house. More opportunities to work. More opportunities to be independent. We've got sass. We've got attitude."

"How do the *guys* take that?"

"As you'd expect, they don't like it. They feel threatened. I mean, look, all their precious women… running amok and too independent. They don't like that at all."

She sighed. "They try to get their revenge. They go back to Iran to find 'proper' Iranian wives, but that usually doesn't work. So then they end up having affairs. They cheat on us. But it's no big deal. We usually end up catching them." She took another drink. "Did you know that Persian women are some of the leading employers of undercover detectives in LA?"

"No."

"Well, they are. There's been a boom in demand. They need them to catch all those cheating husbands. They can get up to their mischief," she said "… but we catch them in the end."

She leaned back in her chair, smiling. "You look puzzled," she said.

"Well–" Josh began.

"Don't worry. It's quite a lot to take in. You've got to remember, you're in LA now. It's a different place altogether."

They fell into silence. The waiters had stopped work now. All the chairs were up on the tables. There was just the sound of glasses being placed on shelves, and the gentle whirr of a dishwasher coming from the kitchen.

Bita drank the last of her wine. "Well," she said. "It's getting late. I think I better be going. I hope that was a useful conversation."

"Absolutely," Josh said.

She pushed her chair back, stood up, and picked up her black leather jacket and bag. As she put her jacket on, she turned to him. "Just out of interest, why did you come to LA?"

"No reason…" Josh began.

She looked at him more closely. "Just… be careful," she said.

"They don't call it the city of broken dreams for nothing."

She slung her bag over her shoulder, pushed her chair in under the table, and left.

Chapter 15

A few weeks passed. The sun continued to beat down as LA edged into autumn. On the mountainsides around the city, forest fires blazed and, down on the streets, the Santa Ana winds gusted in from the eastern desert. Stepping out onto the parched sidewalk was like being blasted by the heat from a red-hot oven.

Josh spent his days cycling around the city. He thought about what the psychologist had said. Maybe he would have to adjust his strategy and adapt to West Coast living. It *was* a different way of life out here. It was very open; you could meet people and be best friends instantly. But then the friendships withered away and vanished. And what could he do about transport? Noushin had told him he needed a car, but he was broke. He simply couldn't afford one.

At moments, he thought of Yasmin. Where was she now? He occasionally allowed himself glimpses at her *Facebook* profile. There weren't many postings, but he could see she was in India. Aside from that he couldn't tell what was happening. The boyfriend appeared in the photos, so he was clearly still on the scene. Josh would curse him and log out hastily.

He spent his evenings searching for jobs. The tedium made his brain numb. Any diversion was welcome. Every single ad or memo that popped onto his screen was a potential distraction.

One evening, it came in the form of a dating website. *Californian Connections* announced itself at the bottom of his screen. After a particularly frustrating day, it was welcome relief. He clicked on the link. *LA's heating up... but is your love life? Find a sizzling date in the LA sunshine. One minute registration, then get browsing!*

It sounded like he was being given the key to some gigantic superstore.

He signed up and created a profile. First, it asked for a photo. No, he thought. Skip that, remain anonymous. But then on second thoughts... why would anyone chat to a faceless profile? He skimmed through his *Facebook* pictures and settled for one where he felt his chest and biceps looked respectable, but not in a showy-off way.

Then all he had to do was choose a username. JoshLA. LostInLA. LoserInLA. That's what he felt like. No, something enticing, something unusual, something… different. Mr… Jigar. MrLiver. Someone Iranian out there might get it. And, for anyone else, it would at least make a good conversation point. He typed it in and hit return triumphantly.

Now, the website announced, *start searching for romance.*

And he was off, trolley in hand, racing down the aisles of the supermarket. As he delved into the profiles, he was quickly engrossed. It was like being given people's private diaries. You could read them for hours and hours. There were the ones who felt sorry for themselves, the pretentious ones, the really genuine and heartfelt ones where he wanted to reach out and hug them right that moment, the scary ones who barely said anything and just glowered at you in the photos.

One girl had described herself as 'curvaceous' followed up with an asterisk at the bottom of the page: **I feel the need to clarify curvaceous isn't a euphemism for fat. I'm about a size ten, just not straight up and down.*

Another one said: *Dislikes: sultanas with rice, awful reality TV, people who hold their knives like pencils, dark mornings and you—if you read this far and don't message me.*

Or people who just posted endless questions: *When you get take-out food, do you eat out of the dishes or transfer the food onto plates? Do you find that the majority of people you happen to encounter, you loathe or dislike tremendously? When you're on your own, have you ever secretly tried to move something with your own mind?*

He moved on. He was browsing a bit further when something flashed up at the bottom of his screen. It was an alert for a new message. He clicked, a flutter of excitement in his stomach.

Hey MrLiver. Welcome to Californian Connections. I see you've only just joined. Hope you're enjoying it so far. A few housekeeping notes…

An auto-message. He let out a deflated sigh and went back to browsing profiles. But, moments later, another message dropped into his inbox.

Hi MrLiver. You haven't written much on your profile. Tell me something about yourself.

Josh re-read the message. It came from a *MissRose*. He clicked on the profile to take a look. There weren't many pictures, just a few shots of her out in the countryside, in rolling green valleys, with snow-capped mountains in the distance.

Then he read her profile. Like his, it was brief.

Hi. Just arrived in LA. Looking to meet a companion in the city of Angels. But be patient–my English is not that great!

Well, he thought, no harm in sending a message.

Nice to 'meet' you... he started writing. *You don't say much either. What's your story?*

A few moments later, a reply came.

That would be telling...

He typed back. *Haha. Well we can't just sit here in silence...*

He waited a moment, then a new message appeared.

I just recently came to LA. Would be nice to meet new people. You?

Pretty much the same, he wrote. *Came here last month. Finding everyone incredibly friendly but it's hard to actually make friends. If you see what I mean.*

Seems like we have the same problem!

Josh paused, figuring out what to write. What was the next step? Just ask her out on a date? What was the etiquette on these things?

Then another message came through.

So why don't we meet in person?

Well, he thought, that took the pain out of that decision.

He typed back. *OK. I think I have enough evidence to show you're not a psychopath. And even if you are... what the heck. Let's do it.*

Meet over a drink? came her answer.

Right, now he had to actually make a plan. *Sure, I can do that. What are you doing Friday night?*

The reply came instantly.

Nothing much...

Well, why don't we meet then?

OK...

I'll have a think about where we could go. What's your scene? He hit SEND and then added some more. *Early evening coffee? Sophisticated bar? Just go straight to a club?!*

There was a moment before her reply came through.

I'm open to anything.

OK. That narrows it down nicely...

She wrote back. *But actually, there's a good gig happening on Friday.*

Where's that?

I think it's near Downtown.

Well if you want to go I'm up for it.

There was a brief pause. The icon spun around to indicate that she was writing. He looked back at her photos, then her new message popped through.

Good. I tell you what, how about we meet at nine and head there together?

He wrote back. *OK. I'll come and pick you up then. Sound good?*

Yeah. I'll see you Friday at nine.

Cool. He hit SEND, and was just about to close his computer when something occurred to him.

Hang on, what's your name?

The icon started spinning. She was still there.

Gabby.

There was a moment before the rest of the message arrived.

And you are... MrLiver?

Well, Josh, in real life.

OK Josh. See you Friday.

See you then.

And, as he hit return, his immediate thought was how on earth he would pick Gabby up when he didn't even have a car.

Chapter 16

Josh spent the rest of the week waiting around in anticipation for the date. Then, when Friday arrived, he spent most of the day getting ready. He ironed a shirt. He shaved. He bought some special waxy stuff–the thing hairdressers ambiguously call 'product'–to put in his hair.

Nima was downstairs in the garden reading a book: *Perfect Italian in a Month.*

"Nima, can I ask you a favor?"

"Sure…"

"Would it be possible to borrow your car?"

He put the book down. "Are you going on a date?"

"Yes."

"Then be my guest. It's nothing special. But I changed the numbers on the back to make it a bit classier."

"What do you mean?"

"It's a *Mercedes.* But only a *150.* So I changed them to *500.* Looks better…"

"Nima, that's a bit weird."

"Don't worry. It's a Persian thing. We all do it. Anyway, where are you going?"

"A gig. It was her suggestion. Don't know what it's going to be like."

"Another Persian girl?"

"Not sure. Possibly."

"What's her name?"

"Gabby."

"Doesn't sound very Persian to me," he said, picking up his book. "Anyway, good luck."

* * *

The evening traffic was light and Josh arrived in West Hollywood shortly before nine. Pulling up at the apartment, he stopped in the orange glow of a street lamp. Gabby was already waiting down on the street. He leaned across and opened the passenger door.

As she climbed in the front seat, Josh leaned forward to kiss her cheek. As he did so she put out her hand. Unfortunately, he saw it too late. He stayed leaning forward to hug her, but put his arm out and shook her hand at the same time, caught halfway between a kiss and a handshake.

"Hey," he said.

"Hi."

Subtly, he tried to take in her appearance. She looked like she had stepped out of the 1980s, as if she had raided her mom's wardrobe. She was wearing a baggy jumper, leggings with a skirt over the top and a belt with a big buckle. On her feet, she wore little boots, and she had large, round earrings and thick-lens glasses that magnified her eyes, as if he were looking at her through a fish tank. They were so heavy that, every so often, they slipped down her nose, and she had to prod them back into place. But, beneath the glasses, she was pretty–bright sparkling eyes, a mole above her upper lip, an awkward but warm smile.

"Thanks for picking me up."

"No problem. I guess you've only just arrived in LA?"

"Yep. No car yet."

"So how do you get around?"

"With great difficulty," she said.

They laughed.

Josh hadn't quite got the hang of Nima's car yet. He heaved the hand brake down, tentatively pushed his foot on the gas, then a little harder, until they jerked forward. They moved off slowly as the car whirred into action, then he dabbed at the gas pedal. It suddenly connected and they surged forward, zipping down the hill in a sudden burst. He noticed Gabby holding onto the passenger door. He wanted to lean back casually, the way drivers do in TV commercials but, instead, he perched on the edge of the seat, hunched over the wheel, to stay in control.

From West Hollywood, they drove south and joined the freeway going east. Once they were coasting along at speed, he could relax a little. He sat back in his seat and loosened his grip on the steering wheel. Finally, he risked speaking.

"So we're heading towards Downtown, right?"

"Yes. I'll tell you when to exit."

"Great. And, sorry if I don't chat. Typical guy–can only do one thing at a time."

They fell back into silence. The freeway was quiet. Looking over his shoulder, he checked for traffic, indicated, then moved over into the fast lane. The radio was on lightly in the background and now a new song came on.

"You know this song?" Gabby said, prodding her glasses back into place.

Josh cocked his head to listen for a moment. "No."

"It's great. My favorite."

She pushed the volume button until the music filled the car. It was some kind of pop song–cheesy but quite catchy. They hummed along the freeway, Gabby bouncing along in her seat and mouthing the music, bobbing her head from side to side.

The traffic was light. They made good time, gliding through the city like an air bubble floating up through a glass of lemonade. Soon, in front of them, the skyscrapers of Downtown appeared, looming, twinkling in the dark. Then, an exit sign for Vermont Avenue flashed past.

"Ah," Gabby said. "I think that's–"

"The exit?"

"Yes."

Josh glanced in the rear mirror, breathed in sharply, and turned hard to the right. Everything seemed to slow down and he watched, paralyzed, as they crossed three lanes of traffic. Then suddenly, miraculously, they were on the slip road, gently decelerating down a curving ramp, like a grand prix car leaving the racetrack, into the pit lane for repairs.

The road they emerged onto was dark and deserted–a wasteland of building sites, car repair shops, and derelict warehouses. Police sirens howled like jackals somewhere in the distance. Gabby pointed to something on their left.

"There," she said.

Josh steered into the center, halting to make a left turn. Then, with a small break in the traffic, he stabbed his foot down onto the gas and darted across the road. On the other side, they came to a sudden, jerky halt.

"Oh geez..."

"I know. Parking nightmare."

They sat stationary. No movement up ahead. Drivers leaned out of their windows, yelling at each other, the air a cacophony of honking and shouting. Josh suddenly felt relieved that he was in a *Mercedes 500*. There were *Porsche Turbos* popping and whopping, *Ferrari*s squealing into wheel spins, white open-top *BMW*s with matching white hubcaps, customized *Bentley*s with personalized number plates, *Rolls-Royce*s with low suspension and tinted windows. And pop music came booming from every single one. It was like they'd inadvertently stumbled into a hot rod contest for the world's most luxurious supercars.

They stood, motionless, waiting in line for the jam to move. Then Josh suddenly spotted a space. Heaving the steering wheel hard to the left, he darted out of the line, through some narrow gaps between parked cars, and into a slender space. He turned off the engine and breathed a sigh of relief.

"Nice one," Gabby said.

"Right. Let's go."

The car park was thick with exhaust fumes, hanging in the air like smog. As they walked across the asphalt, the shriek of breaking car tires ripped through the darkness as people scrambled to find parking spaces.

They joined the queue outside. Josh glanced up and down at the other people. The guys wore white dinner jackets and gold chains the size of boxers' medals. Their shoes were polished so hard they were practically reflective. Their quiffs rippled in the evening breeze. Half of them were wearing shades even though it was the middle of the night. The girls balanced precariously on slender high heels and wore skirts covered in sequins. The cologne and perfume had been lashed on so heavily that the air was thick and almost burned their throats.

They paid the entrance fee and a bouncer rubber-stamped the backs of their hands. Inside, they passed along a corridor of mirrors before arriving at the main performance space. The floor was black beneath their feet, smoke swirled through the air and blue lights twirled above. On the stage sat a drum kit and other instruments, looming in the smoky light.

"Drink?" Josh said.

All of a sudden Gabby looked embarrassed. "Well," she said, hesitantly, "I don't actually drink."

Josh looked blank.

"I mean, not alcohol."

"Oh, right. That's OK…"

"Sorry if that's a problem…"

"No, no problem," he said.

"So, just a soft drink of some kind, please."

"Sure. Give me a minute and I'll get the 'drinks'," he said, putting 'drinks' in mock abbreviation marks with his fingers, feeling like an idiot the moment he did so.

The bar was long and metallic. He picked up a menu card and scanned the cocktails. Melon juice and vodka, raisin vodka, vodka and pomegranate, vodka and rosewater… Josh ordered a melon vodka for himself and juice for Gabby.

"Pomegranate," he said, arriving back beside her.

"And for yourself?"

"Melon vodka, apparently. Never had it before."

They stood and looked around the club while sipping their drinks, like two shy kids not yet comfortable talking to each other. The dance floor was starting to fill up, expectant chat filling the air and more bodies milling around in the dark, the odd person wearing white shining out luminously. Then a voice came from over their shoulders.

"Golnaz. *Chetoree*…?"

Josh turned to see a girl standing behind them.

"*Joonam*! So long since I saw you. *Khubi*?"

"*Man khubam, merci. Tu chetori*?"

"*Khubam, khubam*." The girl came forward. There were hugs, and a busy exchange of kisses.

"Josh," Gabby said. "This is Anahita. Anahita, Josh."

Anahita suddenly stopped talking. She stood motionless and looked at Josh. She gave him a quick studied look, then she smiled.

"Hi," she said. "Nice to meet you."

He took her hand and shook it.

"So," Anahita said, turning back to Gabby, "what you doing

here? I didn't think this was your cup of tea."

"No, no, I love these guys. When I heard they were playing here..."

"Oh sure... well it's their first time. Everyone's been going crazy about it. Anyway, I'm just going upstairs. I'm with some friends in the VIP area. Come join us?"

"Yeah, maybe."

"OK, well, lovely seeing you." She blew kisses and cast a slightly ambiguous look towards Josh. He couldn't tell if it was curiosity or disapproval. "Be careful, don't go too wild tonight." Then she turned and headed off.

"So," Josh said. "Your real name is actually Golnaz?"

"Oh, yeah..."

"You never said you were Iranian."

"I didn't think it was important."

On stage, figures started to appear in the smoky darkness. They looked like a bunch of hippies who had stepped off an ashram; long beards, bandanas, flowery clothing, glittering jewelry. They each took their places at their instruments, the drummer picking up his sticks, the guitarists lifting the guitars from their stands.

The drummer sat hunched over his drum kit, poised, twiddling his sticks. The guitarists strummed the odd chord. Then another man came bounding on from the side of the stage. He plucked the microphone from its stand and a white spotlight hovered around then settled on him. The crowd cheered and applauded.

"Yo! Wassup Los Angeles! Say what, say what, say what...!"

The crowd burst into applause and whoops. The drummer tapped his sticks together and the band sparked into life.

Josh listened for a moment, trying to catch the lyrics, but he couldn't grasp anything. "What do the words mean?" he said into Golnaz's ear above the noise.

"It's about lost love," she said. "Almond eyes... peachy lips... moon-white skin..."

"Oh, nice."

"Kind of..." she said, taking a break from sipping her pomegranate. "But all Persian pop songs have those lyrics. It's sort of boring, actually." She resumed sipping her juice through a straw, bopping her head from side to side.

The song came to an end and the singer turned to the crowd again. "So, guys… thanks for coming out tonight. Big up to everyone in Tehrangeles. We may not be in Iran but we still know what *heyvoon-bazi* means, right?"

The crowd hooted their approval. The singer turned around to face the band, raising his arms like a kind of Christ figure. They launched into the next song.

Josh turned to Golnaz. "So, these guys are Iranian?"

"Yep. What do you think?"

Josh wasn't sure what to say. The beat was difficult to get into. "It's great," he said. "Just a little… unfamiliar."

He turned back to face the band. He nodded his head and tried to get into the rhythm, but there was something strange about the beat that defied him. Golnaz was still bopping along, so he felt he ought to try harder. He finished his drink, put his glass down, and tried to ease himself into a few moves of his own. He gently started stepping from side to side and swinging his arms. He felt awkward at first–robotic–consciously trying to coordinate his movements to the beat.

"So, what kind of music is this exactly?"

"I guess you'd call it Persian pop."

"What does that mean?"

"It means it's a bit weird, but Persians like it."

"OK, if we're listening to Persian pop, you ought to teach me some Persian dance moves."

Golnaz laughed. "Well, this is one." She angled her body to the side and shuffled around like she was scattering seeds in a field.

"Ah. The seeding farmer. That's pretty easy."

"Right," she said. "Your turn."

"Well, I used to know how to tango."

"Oh great. Teach me."

"You plant your hand on my back, like this." He took her hand and placed it on the small of his back. "And with your other hand…" he took her right hand in his left. "And now it's two basic steps: slow-slow… quick-quick. And again… slow-slow, quick-quick.”

They began to glide across the dance floor. Suddenly, they hit a pause in the music, and froze their position. He leaned forward and she leaned back with him.

“Except,” he said, “you’re not really meant to look into each other’s eyes.”

At that moment, the song ended. They eased out of position and let go of each other. The crowd burst into applause and they joined the clapping.

They retired to the edge of the dance floor while the band played another few songs, then the singer addressed the crowd. “We’re taking a short break. Don’t go away, because we’ll be back for more.”

People began to disperse; some to the bar, others outside to smoke. Josh turned to Golnaz to suggest another drink.

“Well, actually, I hate to say this, but I think I’m going to have to call it a night.”

“Oh right, OK.”

“I’ve got an English exam tomorrow. Need to get some sleep ready for some last-minute studying.”

They retrieved their coats from the cloakroom and headed out. Walking through the parking lot, it was quieter now, just row upon row of silent shining cars, like the yard of a supercar dealership after hours. The smoke hung in the air like a thin mist, and they could smell the scent of burned rubber. As they walked across the asphalt, the sound of the band gearing up for their second set echoed from the club.

They arrived at the car and got in quietly. The vodka had been strong but Josh felt his head was just clear enough to drive. He pulled out of their space and they purred off in silence.

Golnaz turned to Josh. “You enjoyed it?”

“It was great. My first Persian gig.”

“Good. I’m glad.”

There was a moment’s silence. They continued to drive.

“So, I never asked you,” he said. “You grew up in Iran?”

“Yes.”

“And when did you move here?”

“Last year, after I finished my undergrad.”

"Only last year? Your English is pretty good."

"I listened to American music when I was little. And watched American films."

Josh looked out of the car window at the traffic opposite. The road east was bumper to bumper, but going west it wasn't too bad. They cruised with that peculiar sense of relief you get while racing past a traffic jam on the other side of the freeway.

"And how do you like life in Tehrangeles?"

She smiled. "Tehrangeles. You call it that?"

"I thought that's what it was called."

"It is. But it's the first time I've heard a foreigner say it." She looked out of the window for a moment. "Well, it's strange. I mean, it's full of Iranians. It's like a mini-Iran. But it's not like real Iran."

"How do you mean?"

"It feels so... *old*. Like it's the 1970s or something. The shop names. What people say. People still use the old phone codes from back in Iran."

"That's weird."

"And the way people speak–the young people. Most of them haven't been to Iran. So their language–it sounds funny. Like my parents'."

Josh changed lanes. "And what do they think of you?"

"Oh, they find me funny, too. They say *I* speak strange. And some of them look at me and say, *oh, she's a FOB.*"

"FOB?"

"*Fresh off the boat.* You know, silly immigrant. Doesn't know anything. Un... un... how do you say?"

"Unsophisticated?"

"Yes. *Unsophisticated.* They make fun of me. Like my accent. I say Vestvood instead of Westwood. Things like that."

"But your accent's OK..."

"I know. It is *now*. But when I arrived, it was different. When I first opened my mouth here I thought: Hhmm, I better lose *that*."

The streets were quiet now. The palm trees stood silhouetted against a dusky sky. An orange glow rose off the city, like a silent inferno burned all around.

"But not everyone makes fun of FOBs," she said, after a pause. "Some people… they have respect. They look at me and say, *ooo, she's a proper Iranian*. She's been on Iranian land. Eaten Iranian food. Breathed Iranian air. She is real *Irooni*."

"They're jealous?"

"Not *jealous*. More, they don't feel *real*. They want to be real Iranians. But they've never been. So they can't."

They continued in silence for a while. Then, after passing Fairfax, they turned off the freeway and onto the surface roads. The speed of the freeway subsided into the background. Soon they were back in West Hollywood. Up until this point, it had felt like the evening was winding down. But now, as they got closer to the house, the energy returned. A tension rose in the car.

"Just here," Golnaz said.

He pulled up at the apartment block, then stopped the car. He was about to turn off the engine, hesitated in case it looked presumptuous, then did it anyway.

"So," he said. "Here we are."

During the drive, Josh had been wondering how the night would end. Would they just say a friendly goodbye? Would there be a kiss on the cheek? Or maybe a proper kiss? He wasn't sure. They had gotten along OK. But he couldn't tell what Golnaz was expecting. To be frank, he didn't know whether she had seen this as a date or not.

They sat for a few moments in the dark.

"So, Golnaz. That was a really lovely evening."

"Yes. I had a great time. Thank you."

"We should do it again sometime."

"Yes," she said. "We should."

There was another silence. Josh tried to think of something to say but his mind had run dry. He wouldn't be able to maintain this much longer. At some point, he'd have to take the plunge and make a move. He turned sideways to face Golnaz. She seemed to stiffen slightly. He'd seen this moment hundreds of times in films and TV but, in reality, he thought to himself, there is no way to turn and face someone in a car at the end of a date and *not* make it look like you plan to kiss them.

"So," he said, trying to shift her attention to something else. "Maybe we could go to another gig…"

"Yes…"

"Or maybe something else…"

"Sure…"

He was fumbling now. Conversation had ended. This was it. He paused for one final moment, mentally bracing himself, like a diver at the top of the highest board. He took one last breath in.

Then all of a sudden, he felt himself flung against the car door. Golnaz was pressed up against him and the back of his head was jammed against the window. Everything seemed to go hazy, but he had the distinct feeling that an eel had been released into his mouth. Josh kept trying to subdue it with his tongue but its frantic squirming was uncontrollable. He chased for a few moments, then gave up and allowed it free reign. Finally, it ran out of energy and, after a few sporadic bursts of movement, it seemed to die a natural death and retreat.

He slumped back down into the seat. Golnaz slid back to her side of the car, and prodded her glasses back into place with her finger. Josh remained in the passenger seat, looking straight out through the front windscreen.

There was a long pause. The only noise was the sound of their breathing.

"*Khub*," she said. "I better be going." She looked out through the windscreen. "I'll see you around."

She reached for the handle, opened the door, and got out. Then, without leaning back down to say goodbye, she closed the door with a thud and he listened to the sound of her footsteps as she disappeared up to the apartment.

Josh sat in the car, now in total silence. After a few minutes, he turned on the ignition. It purred quietly into life. The front headlamps came on, casting their beam ahead, insects dancing in the light. He reversed slightly, then shifted gear and began to pull away. The wheels squeaked as they turned against the asphalt and he began to drive back down the empty street.

Chapter 17

Josh awoke late the next morning. The sun was already high in the sky, light beaming down through the windows, flooding into his bedroom. He lay in bed in that contented state between sleep and wakefulness, running over the previous night's events in his mind: the club, the journey home... the kiss.

The kiss. Of all the kisses he had experienced, it had undoubtedly been the most bizarre. It had come completely out of the blue, and it had been so... surreal. He touched his lips as if to check that it had been real. As he lay in bed, he wondered whether it had happened at all, until he'd thought about it so much that he really *did* wonder whether it had happened at all.

After replaying it in his head a few times, and finally convincing himself that it had really happened, he heaved himself out of bed and dragged his body downstairs to the garden.

Nima was there, sitting at a table, drinking coffee, working on his laptop.

"Hey, Mr. Loverman. Good night?"

"Yes," Josh said in a slight daze. "Yes... it was a good one."

Nima raised his eyebrows. "That all you're going to say?"

"For now..."

"The car was OK?"

"Fine. You saved me there. I owe you one."

Josh settled into a chair and sat staring at the flowers. He picked up his phone and started skimming through his inbox. He half thought there might be a message from Golnaz, but there wasn't. He decided to send her one himself.

Hey Golnaz. You ok? Great night yesterday. Loved the band. Let's do it again sometime. J x

He put the phone down and sat staring vacantly at the flowers for a while, then turned around to Nima.

In the last few weeks, Josh had noticed another change in Nima's appearance. Gone was the Italian look. Now he was wearing more sober suits, brightly colored ties, and polished shoes. He even had a new hairstyle–a side-parting–and he was clean shaven.

"What's with the change of image, Nima?"

"My new initiative."

"Which is?"

"Politics."

"Yeah?"

"Yes. Local politics." He pulled out a poster. There was a picture of Nima, standing in front of his garden, beaming a huge smile. *Nima: Man of Action, not a Dreamer* ran the slogan at the bottom.

"The problem is," Nima said, "I need money."

"For what?"

"To fund my campaign. I'm going to a party in Beverly Hills tomorrow. Obscenely rich people. Chance to schmooze. Maybe they'll give me some money."

"Good luck."

"If you want, you could come along, too. It's Persian. It'll be interesting for you. Lots of chances to meet young, rich Persian women. And I mean, *rich*."

"Well, I'd love to, but I think I'm catered for in that department now."

"No, come on. You'll have fun."

Josh thought to himself. He'd done quite a bit of partying recently. He felt he needed a break. But there probably wasn't any harm in just going to one more.

"Well," he said, "I guess I could pop along briefly."

***

Sunday evening rolled around. Nima was heading to the party from a meeting in town with potential donors to his campaign, so he had given Josh the address and told him to make his own way there.

It was already dark when Josh set off on his bike. He pedaled along the six-lane immensity of Wilshire Boulevard, the traffic tearing past him, like a flea amidst a herd of elephants. Soon, he was in Beverly Hills, passing along the dark boulevards and empty sidewalks. From the shopping arcades up into the residential areas, everything was still, the streets empty and silent. The enormous palm trees rose high into the air, motionless against the night sky. The mansions stood along the street like ghoulish fairy-tale castles, partially hidden behind foreboding walls, lights shimmering and flickering in the dark.

The address was in the higher reaches of Beverly Hills, up towards Bel Air. Josh pedaled onwards and upwards, hunched over the handle bars like he was doing a mountain section of the *Tour de France*. The road seemed to go on forever, winding further up, the gradient getting steeper and steeper, past one driveway after another.

Eventually, he arrived. He locked his bike to the railings out the front and began walking up the drive, the scrunch of his shoes on the gravel the only sound in the night air. As the house loomed up in front of him, he felt like a medieval peasant approaching some kind of impregnable fortress. Along the pathway stood gaudy statues and monumental hedges in weird, fantastical shapes; enormous lions and fantasy beasts looming sinisterly in the gloom.

The front door was flanked by two enormous fluted columns. Josh rang the bell and waited. The gentle murmur of conversation drifted from behind the curtains in the illuminated rooms. Eventually, he heard footsteps, and the door opened.

A woman stood before him wearing black, a champagne glass in her hand, as an artist might hold a paintbrush. Her silk dress rippled in the light, and around her throat was a glittering necklace, like she had stepped out of a diamond advert. Josh stood on the doorstep, soaked with sweat, flattening his hair now that his bike helmet was off.

There was a moment's pause as they looked at each other, then the woman broke into an enormous beaming smile.

"Ah, you must be Josh, Nima's friend? I'm Fereshteh. Salaam."

"Salaam," Josh said. He stepped through the door into the entrance hall, tall enough for a giraffe to stand up in. Fereshteh gave him a kiss on each cheek as she held her glass aloft with her free hand.

"A small gift," he said, handing over a bottle of wine he had brought.

"Och, joonam," Fereshteh said. "You shouldn't have. Really. How kind of you."

She took the bottle, then looked down at the bicycle helmet in his other hand.

"And what is this?" she said, a look of beguiled curiosity on her face.

"My bike helmet."

There was a pause as Fereshteh looked down at the bike helmet.

"But Josh, you don't need this. It's not a costume party!"

"No, I was wearing it. I came by bike."

Fereshteh looked at Josh, searching his face for traces of humor. But after a moment, she realized he was telling the truth.

"You... well. I must tell this to Bahman. Anyway, come," she said. "Nima's here but a bit distracted. Let's get you a drink and I'll introduce you to some people."

She put the bike helmet on the floor, took him by the arm, and led him in. They walked through the hall, past statues of Greek gods and goddesses, the white marble so pristine it looked fake, like artificially whitened teeth.

Through into the main room, they passed across densely woven carpets, like in pictures of mosques he'd seen in *National Geographic* magazine. Around the room were gleaming white couches, and at one end stood a glass table laden with food.

Fereshteh waltzed through, gliding past a small fountain. Then she led him by the hand towards some guests.

"Nima is over there, wooing people for his political campaign." Josh looked over to where she was pointing. He saw Nima, busily talking to a group of men in suits. He heard the words drifting over: "Vote for Nima...man of action, not a dreamer..."

"Come," said Fereshteh. "I will introduce you."

She led him to a group of middle-aged men and women at one side of the room. They wore suits and ball gowns, the women dripping in jewelry, with severe black-painted eyebrows and perfectly straight black hair. They wore so much makeup it was difficult to tell their age–they could have been anything between 20 and 50.

"Everyone," Fereshteh said. "Meet Josh. He came by bike!"

There was a moment of silence. The people stopped talking and looked at Josh. Then everyone burst out laughing.

"Hi," Josh said.

Then he felt Fereshteh's arm tugging at his side. "Come Josh. Into the garden. You must meet more people."

They went back through the entrance hall, in the other direction towards the back of the house. They passed through a dining room, tables groaning with food: platters of rice studded with herbs and berries; piles of roasted meat garnished with sizzling grilled tomatoes; dishes of cucumber, spring onion, and leafy, freshly-washed herbs and salads–the colors so bright they looked unnatural. Finally, in the middle, the centerpiece: a chocolate fountain, spouting out a gentle river of molten dark chocolate, thick and warm.

At the end of the dining room, they passed through sliding doors out onto an expanse of wooden decking. The nighttime air was cool and the steady sound of crickets chirping came from the hills around them. Josh walked over to the edge of the deck; beneath them extended an enormous garden, all in shadow. The one source of light was a shimmering swimming pool, the iridescent turquoise water rippling and reflecting the lights from the house. Beyond the silhouetted trees, the Santa Monica Mountains were a dark immensity studded with lights.

A small group of guests stood on the deck overlooking the garden. Fereshteh led him towards them.

"Everyone," she said, arriving at their side. "Meet Josh. He came by bike."

Everyone looked around. There was the same moment of silence as before–a wave of curiosity passing over them. Then they burst into laughter. Josh waited until it stopped and everyone was quiet again.

"Did you actually cycle?"

"How was the ride?"

Behind him, more guests were arriving. The deck was filling up, and there was a rising noise of clinking glasses and conversation.

"Come," Fereshteh said. "We must get you a drink."

She led Josh back inside and into another room where a bar was set up against one of the walls.

"You can have anything you like. Why don't you try the cocktails? They're very good."

Feeling like he had stepped onto the set of a *James Bond* film, Josh felt the obvious choice of drink was a martini. As the waiter stood shaking the tumbler full of ice, Fereshteh spotted someone across the room.

"Josh, will you excuse me a moment? There's someone I must speak to."

She picked her glass up off the bar and glided over to the other side of the room. Josh turned to find his drink was ready. He picked it up to take a sip. It was strong and sent a warm intoxicating wave through his body. He stood and surveyed the party.

More guests had arrived now. They stood in clusters around the room. Josh looked among them, searching for a familiar face. Perhaps one of Nima's friends might be here. But he didn't recognize anyone. He continued sipping his drink, leaning against the bar. His mind drifted back to *Bond* movies... this was the moment where a jaw-dropping woman would approach him with a snappy one-liner. He cast his eyes around. There were plenty of jaw-dropping women. But somehow, he didn't feel any of them would approach him. Looking for a distraction, he took his phone out to check for a message from Golnaz, but there was nothing.

He put his phone back in his pocket. He sipped his cocktail. The glass was so wide and low that it took just one gulp to finish it. He put it back down on the bar. The barman happened to be passing at that moment.

"Another one, sir?"

Josh hesitated. It had been quite strong. He could feel its effects kicking in already... but why not? It was free, and the party looked fun. The only problem was that he was on his bike. To hell with that, he thought.

"Sure. One more. Thanks."

The barman left and prepared the drink. Josh stood surveying the party, listening to the slush of liquid as the barman shook the tumbler, the thud as he released the glass from the mixer, and the satisfying fizz as it filled the glass.

"There you go, sir."

Josh took a long sip. The first drink had started to take effect now and he was getting light-headed. The second sip sent another pulse through his body. He took another and a satisfying dullness enveloped him.

He finished the drink. Looking out from the bar, he realized he definitely felt wobbly now. The room spun slowly around him, the high ceilings as far above him as the night sky. The house seemed cavernous, conversation echoing around the walls like he was in a church. He looked around at the people. Which were shinier, he thought to himself… the faces or the bronzed roast chickens? The women tottered on high heels, bosoms bulging out of their dresses, caked in makeup. One carried a white poodle grasped firmly in her arm. They cast insecure glances at each other's hair and nails, wondering whose teeth were whitest, and their eyes were heavy with mascara, welling up in tiny clumps if you looked close, like little bits of coal hanging from their eyelashes. So many air kisses had been blown, the air itself seemed to be blushing.

Feeling the need to sober up, he walked to the back of the house and out onto the deck. The cool air was refreshing and he looked up at the vast, deep, black sky, peppered with stars, perfect white glimmers of light.

He took out his phone, still wondering if there was a message from Golnaz. He scrolled down through his inbox, the little screen casting a blue light against his face, but there was nothing. She'd had the whole day to reply. Why the silence?

Suddenly, Josh shivered. Standing out on the deck, the chatter and laughter echoing from within, he felt a powerful wave of nausea rise up inside him. The whole landscape seemed to sway and ripple, as if buckling from an earthquake. He staggered slightly, grabbing at the handrail to steady him.

He stood for a moment, holding onto the handrail, until he felt secure, taking deep lungfuls of air. Then, he turned slowly, and began to walk back through the house. He passed through the rooms of chattering guests, the sound of clinking glasses and conversation, and in the background, the steady flow of molten chocolate.

Exiting through the front door, he passed down the gravel path. The hedges loomed menacingly; the lions that had looked proud and purring now seemed to growl and snarl in the dark. He walked quicker, until he found his bike and unlocked it. He wheeled it out of the driveway, hurrying now, as if he were being pursued.

He got on and started pedaling. Away in the night sky, the moon sat high and proud, a perfect white ball in a white-pricked black ocean. And he cycled homewards, back through the empty, silent streets, the chilled night air cool against his flushed skin.

Chapter 18

For the second time in three days, Josh woke late. This time, as he looked at his watch, he saw it was already approaching midday.

He hauled himself out of bed. For a moment, as he stood up, he felt fresh and revived. Then, within seconds, the blood seemed to drain through his body and out from his feet. Light-headedness overcame him and he crawled back into bed. As he lay there, his temples throbbed. His throat was parched and rancid.

He lay in bed until he could survive no longer without water, then he hobbled downstairs, glugged as much as his stomach would take, staggered into the garden like a zombie, and collapsed into a chair in a crumpled heap. A cool breeze filtered through the garden and offered some refreshment, but the gruesome dull ache in his head did not abate.

Needing some distraction, he took out his phone. He checked his emails–nothing. He browsed *Facebook*–nothing. Then he checked his texts. He wondered if there might be something from Golnaz. But again–nothing. He closed his eyes and tried not to think about it, then fell back into a lazy early afternoon sleep.

He woke half an hour later with a jolt. Although he still felt rotten, he decided he had to do something with the day. A bike ride. Down to the ocean. Some sea air refreshment–if there was any tonic that would cure him of his ills, that was it.

He tentatively wheeled his bike out into the drive. Climbing on gingerly, he began cruising down the hilly streets of Brentwood. He rattled over the cracks in the street, gentler this time; he felt fragile, not a speed demon today.

He cycled his usual route, down to Santa Monica pier, then walked out across the beach. Stopping to pick up lumps of wet sand, he broke it up with his hands, letting it crumble and fall between his fingers. He did this for a while and it felt therapeutic. Then, when his hands were tired, he lay back on the beach and stared up at the enormous expanse of sky. He closed his eyes and listened to the sweep, heave, and splash of the waves arriving at the shore.

He spent the rest of the afternoon cycling in the districts south of Santa Monica. By late afternoon, the pounding in his head had cleared, but his body was exhausted. His legs felt heavy and his thighs ached. Deciding it was time to head home, he began to cycle back towards Brentwood. Looking up at the sky beyond the Santa Monica Mountains, the sun had disappeared. The sky grew dark as gray clouds massed and threatened rain. Soon, he felt the thud of the first droplets begin to fall.

He began to pedal faster. He passed through Culver City, through the desolate warehouse districts, past endless concrete shacks. The rain grew heavier. Then the heavens opened. Searching for somewhere to pull up and stop, he saw a hotel and skidded to a halt. He took refuge under the awning out the front and looked out across the deserted car park. There is nothing in the world emptier than an empty car park, he thought to himself.

He stood under the awning, the rain falling in heavy droplets on the canvas. He peered through the big window of the hotel into the lobby. It was cold and wet outside, and his body was shivering. Deciding he needed to warm up, he locked up his bike and went inside.

The hotel lobby was heavily carpeted and the air immediately comforting against his skin. He stood for a moment, enjoying the warmth. Then he went into the toilets to find an air blower. He ducked under its warm blast, feeling his hair dry and the shivers retreat.

He went back out into the lobby. Then he noticed them, over to his right: a crowd of people. He was surprised he hadn't seen them on his way in. There were several dozen of them, standing around chatting and drinking tea.

They were dressed formally; the men in suits with silk ties, some with medals, pocket handkerchiefs, and gold cufflinks. The women wore long dresses, heavily laden with jewelry. They were drinking tea, and their conversation produced a gentle murmuring noise along with the clink of teaspoons on teacups. The whole occasion had the air of a lawn bowls convention.

As they stood around talking, a soft voice came over a

loudspeaker, like an announcement at a theater just before the play is about to start. "Ladies and gentlemen, please proceed into the hall. This evening's event will start in a few minutes."

The people began filing out of the waiting area into a hall. Josh looked outside. The rain was lighter now, but it continued to fall. He looked back towards the people streaming into the hall. Curious, he followed them, and slipped quietly into a seat at the back.

Inside, everyone sat down quickly and a hush settled on the room. People stowed their teacups away on the floor beneath their seats. There was a moment of silence. Everyone waited expectantly, then a mobile phone went off. The entire hall burst out tutting. The offender rummaged in their bag and silenced it.

Then the lights in the hall dimmed. A projector whirred into life and threw its beam against the wall at the front, particles of dust dancing in the stream of light. A crackly soundtrack came on, a sort of military theme tune, like a parade ground marching song. Suddenly, everyone stood to attention, as if some dignitary had entered the room.

The specks and particles danced and flickered on the screen. Then a film started to play. Josh watched as a montage of still photographs appeared. He didn't recognize any of the people. There was a man–stern-looking, clean-shaven. He always wore a suit and sometimes dark glasses. He was shown in different poses; on skis, by a military helicopter, with his family. Each shot seemed slightly stiff and unnatural, as if it had been carefully staged.

Meanwhile, the crowd watched. They fell silent, gazing up at the screen. Not even a murmur. The light from the projector threw a glow out across the sea of faces.

The final shot showed the man wearing a white military uniform, heavily laden with medals, a gold and blue sash across his chest. Then the film came to an end. The soundtrack crackled and stopped.

The screen fell dark. Then the projector whirred into life again and threw out a new beam of light. More dust danced in the air, then a face gradually appeared on the screen. At first, it looked eerily like the man from before. He had the same heavy nose and dark brown eyes, similar thick eyebrows, well-groomed and ruddy cheeks. But he was younger, with fewer gray hairs, and less stern. He was sitting at a dark mahogany desk, wearing a dark suit with a white shirt and blue tie. Behind him were large windows looking out onto green lawns.

As he appeared, a ripple of whispers passed through the audience. Gasps from the women. Small grunts of approval from the men. Then the man began to speak.

"My people. We have come together on this important day. Our dynasty may have fallen. Memories grow frail, but we will never forget.

"The time will come. That time when you will return to your spiritual homeland."

"*Ach, joonam*," a woman burst out, before burying her face into her handkerchief.

"Until that day, be strong. Be resolute. Build your stomach for the fight and anticipate the joys that await you when you return.

"I thank you for your support. I may be one, but I act for you all, and we all should act as one. The journey may be long, but it will be an honorable one."

There was silence as he sat at the desk, looking straight ahead. Then, slowly, the screen began to fade. The man's face gradually disappeared and, after a while, the image dissolved to black.

The light from the projector fell away. A darkness descended on the room. Everyone stood, staring at the screen, a sea of silent faces.

Then, very quietly from the back of the hall, there came a sound. At first, it was indistinct; a sort of heaving, wheezing noise. Someone breathing heavily, or sniffing to keep their nose from running. Then the sound began to spread. More people began sniffling. It seemed to move around the room like a contagion.

Soon, the whole room was filled with the sound. It was more than just a sniffling now. It was a convulsing physical wheeze, culminating in a sob–a deep, full-bodied sob. It was uncontrollable. Infectious. With every person it touched, it brought them to their knees.

Handkerchiefs were produced. Noses were blown. Glasses were removed and eyes dabbed. Cheeks turned red and swollen. Lips trembled, as a great collective howl went up, a great wail of noise.

Then, just as this noise began to subside, another sound began–a different sound. It came first from the back of the room. Just a small cry in the big hall. But then it became audible.

"Javid Shah."

"Javid Shah."

Now the first voice was accompanied by a second. And then another, and another. Soon, it had spread all around the room. A chorus of voices. The shout boomed up from the rows of people, reverberating off the walls, shaking the entire room and building.

Josh stood where he was at the back. The room was filled with the desperate shout. *"Javid Shah, javid shah."*

It felt claustrophobic now, almost dangerous, like blood would be spilt. Like a pack of hounds baying for blood. It sent a shiver up his spine, and he decided it was time to leave.

He slipped quietly from the back row, the cries echoing behind him. He went out into the lobby–deserted now–and walked back towards the entrance. He paused at the door and looked out the window. The rain had stopped. He was just about to leave, when he noticed a man standing next to him, staring out of the window onto the car park.

He wore a crumpled suit and had a wild frizz of white hair. Wide eyes. Disturbed face and pale skin. Like that man in the painting, a permanent scream fixed on his face. His thick black glasses magnified his eyes.

There was a moment of silence as they looked at each other.

"Who was that person?" Josh said.

The man looked at him. "The Shah in waiting." His eyes looked into Josh's, but they were vacant, as if he were staring right through him. "The world moved in that moment," he said. "Like it does every year. But still, we are no closer to what we want."

There was silence. The man looked away, through the huge windows, streaked with rain, out across the empty car park, into the dark evening.

Josh turned and left. He passed outside into the car park, from the cozy warmth of the hotel lobby into the cool, fresh air. The rain had stopped now. The asphalt was dotted with puddles, reflecting light from the streetlights. The sky was weak, relieved from emptying its load. There was a calm in the air, just the sound of the last water droplets trickling down from the gutters, running off the hotel awning to the ground.

Suddenly, he thought of Golnaz. He took out his phone and, in the evening gloom, the blue light produced an almost supernatural glow. He checked his inbox. No messages. Then he looked up her number in his contacts and, after a brief hesitation, hit dial.

He held the phone to his ear and listened to the ring tones. One… two… three… it would hit the answering machine soon. He began composing a message in his head.

Then the ring broke off and a voice came down the line.

"Hello?"

"Hi. Is that Golnaz?"

"Yes." There was a pause. "Who's this?"

"It's Josh."

"Josh…"

"Yes. Don't you have…?"

"Oh, Josh. Sorry."

Brief pause.

"How are you?" asked Golnaz.

"I'm fine. How are you?"

"Yeah. I'm OK."

Another pause.

"So," he said, "I was just calling to see how you are."

"I'm fine. Thanks."

"That's good."

"How are you?"

"I'm fine, too, thank you."

Another pause, a little awkward this time.

"So," Josh said. "It's been a funny day. With the weather, I mean. I hope you didn't get too wet."

"No," Golnaz said. "No, I was OK."

"Good. I was about to, but then… well, I was OK."

"About to what?"

"Get wet."

"Oh, right."

Another slight pause.

"So," Josh said. "Did you get my messages?"

"Your messages?"

"I sent you a text. Two, actually. One yesterday, one the day before."

"Oh, right. I may have got them. I haven't really been checking."

"OK, well, don't worry. They weren't anything important. I mean, they just said, well, nothing much actually."

More silence down the line.

"So," Golnaz said. "Was there a reason for your call?"

"Well, no, not really. I mean, you know, just saying hello."

More silence, deeper this time.

"And I guess I just wanted to…"

"Yes?"

"To clarify… exactly…"

"*Yes*?"

"To clarify what the *situation* was between us, exactly."

"The situation?"

"Yes. After the other night. I wasn't sure… what you meant by it."

"The other night?"

"Yes. When you… you know…"

"When, what?"

"When we… when you… when you kissed me."

Another pause.

"I'm sorry?"

"When we kissed. In my car."

"Josh, I'm afraid I don't know what you're talking about."

"When you kissed me. In the front seat of my car."

"Josh…"

"We were sitting there, you were next to me, and you leaned over, and–"

"Josh," Golnaz said, a firmness in her voice now. "I don't

know why you think we kissed."

"Well, I don't think it. I mean, I remember it quite clearly..."

"Because, that's not the kind of thing–"

"I definitely wasn't imagining it..."

"It's really not what I–"

"Well," Josh said, "I think we did actually. I mean, I know it was late and everything, and maybe I'd had a couple of drinks, and you... well, actually, you were totally sober. But, anyway, I do recall what happened."

Pause.

"You don't remember?"

Total silence down the line.

"Josh, I don't have any memory of this."

"I'm sorry?"

"I don't have any memory of a kiss."

"Well, let me see if I can help you. We were driving ba–"

"I think you've made a mistake. I don't think you've remembered right."

"No," Josh said. "Actually, I remember it quite *clearly*. We stopped outside your apartment. It was dark. I turned the engine off. I was just turning to face you to say goodbye, when you *flung* your arms around me, *pinned* me against the door of the car, and kissed me. I am definitely, *definitely*, not imagining that."

A short pause.

"Josh, I don't know what you're talking about. I would never do that."

"What do you mean, you'd never do it? You did it!"

"It's not the kind of thing I do. I don't just kiss people the first time I meet up with–"

"So you're just denying that any of this took place? You're just pretending it never happened?"

"Look, Josh. I don't know what you might have imagined between us. But I'm afraid there isn't anything. I'm sorry."

"This is actually pretty strange..."

"Now, if you'll excuse me, I've got to go."

"I can't quite believe this is–"

"I'm sorry. I don't want to hurt your feelings. But I've got to go. Bye.”

He heard the dull click of the line going dead. Then silence.

Josh brought the phone down from his ear and stood looking for a moment at the screen–dull and lifeless now. For a moment, he couldn't quite believe he'd had that conversation, like when you see a celebrity and you can't be sure it was really true.

He stood there a little longer, then closed the phone, and put it in his pocket. He looked out into the desolate night; the empty car park, the asphalt flooded with water slicks reflecting the street lamp lights, the highway beyond, cars bursting through the puddles, water spraying all around them.

And then, suddenly, he thought of something else. Yasmin. Where was she right now? He could see her face in his mind. Her smile. The glitter beneath her eyes. The gold streaks in her black hair. Her face seemed to glow in his mind like the warmth of a summer evening. Where in the world was she right now?

He stood there in the chill night air, looking up at the dusky orange sky, wondering where she was. And, as he stood, he wondered whether she was out there somewhere, looking up at the same sky he was looking at, seeing the same stars he could see, thinking the same thoughts he was thinking.

Chapter 19

January wore on. The rains continued. The streets flooded and the traffic splashed through the puddles. The sunlit paradise of LA seemed to have disappeared beneath gray skies and perpetual rain clouds.

Josh didn't have much to do. He went on long bike rides, cycling aimlessly around the city. He passed through district after district of LA's never-ending urban landscape, buffeted by the winds from passing trucks. He felt like a ghost, stalking the streets of LA, like his spirit had left his body and floated away.

Sometimes, he headed down to Santa Monica and sat on the beach, staring out across the sand. He remembered the excitement he had felt when he first arrived in the city: the dreams, the energy, the ambition. All that hadn't gone away completely. The little blue huts still gave him a tingle of excitement. But now when he looked at them, he didn't see himself running across the sand. Instead, he was going at more of a jog. And, rather than diving into the sea, he just fell, plopped sideways into the shallows, and waded his way out.

At times, he thought about giving up and going home. There was a life waiting for him back on the East Coast. Sure, it wasn't exciting. Doing accounts in his father's law firm. But at least his family were there. In LA, he felt unloved. Unwanted. He could disappear one day, and no one would even notice.

One evening, he had gotten back home after a whole day cycling around the city. He was sitting at the table in the garden, looking at his computer, still pursuing his fruitless search for a job. Nima was there, too, lying in a hammock, drinking a glass of orange juice with turmeric and ginger.

"Nima, you know I asked you before why everyone in LA was Iranian…"

"Yes."

"And, you said it was because we were in Tehrangeles…"

"Yes."

"Well, I've been thinking. I actually think everyone in LA *is* Iranian."

Nima laughed.

"I mean, everyone I meet here is from Iran."

"Like?"

"Like... my friend's friend. Your friends. That therapist. The girl from the dating site..."

"I think you just seem to attract Iranians."

"What do you mean?"

"I think you're obsessed with Tehrangeles. Didn't you meet some girl? Back home?"

"No..."

"I thought you mentioned her."

"Nah..."

"I think you're chasing some kind of ghost."

Josh looked away. "No," he said, "it's nothing to do with that."

They fell into silence. Josh hadn't chatted to Nima much recently. He wasn't sure what was happening with his political campaign. But he had noticed that he was no longer leaving the house each day in his shiny suit, and he was taking fewer 'high status' calls than before.

"Oh, by the way, Josh," Nima said after a while, "I was thinking... what exactly are you planning on doing out here in LA? For work, I mean."

"That's an issue, Nima. I need to find some. Fast. My bank balance is looking pretty unhealthy."

"What kind of thing are you looking for?"

"I'll do anything. As long as it's legal."

"Well," he took a sip of his drink and placed it on the ground. "There was something going the other day that might be of interest. I was chatting to a friend. There might be an opening with his company."

"Did you tell him about me?"

"Sure, I mentioned you. Lost and lonely vagrant, newly arrived in LA. Destitute and in need of work. They said it sounded like a good fit." Nima produced a business card from his pocket. "Here's the number."

Josh took the card. *Telikani-Rezvani Associates. LA real estate.* "Nima, I don't know the first thing about real estate–"

"Neither do they. That's why you'd fit in. Give them a call now, before you lose the chance."

Josh went to a quiet part of the garden and looked at the card. It was decorated with winged mythological figures and a slogan at the bottom said: *Don't count the bedrooms, count the columns!*

He picked up his phone and dialed the number. It rang a few times, then a woman answered.

"Telikani-Rezvani..."

"Hello. I wondered if I could speak to–" he looked down at the card "–Farhad Latifi?"

"Farhad?"

"Yes."

"You mean *Fred*?"

"Well, it says Farhad on the card."

"I think you mean Fred. I'll see if he's in."

The line went dead. A few moments later, the voice returned.

"I'm afraid Fred can't come to the phone right now. But I can take a message, if you like?"

"Could you tell him that Josh called? Josh Mayhew. I was given his number by Nima Rahimi."

"Oh, hang on. Are you...? I think someone mentioned you."

She put the phone back down then, a few seconds later, she picked up again.

"Hello, Josh? I just spoke to Fred. He's busy and can't talk right now. But he wondered if you could come into the office sometime."

"Sure. When was he thinking?"

"Are you free tomorrow?"

"Yes, I could do that. What time?"

"Two?"

"That works for me."

"OK. We'll see you then. You've got our address? When you reach the fifteenth floor, turn left, look for the fountain, and you're there."

"Thanks." Josh hung up.

"Nima," he said. "Are these guys Iranian, too?"

Nima smiled. "You betcha!"

The next day was cool and hazy. It had rained during the night and the streets were wet, with little puddles dotting the sidewalk. Pedestrians hurried around them and buses splashed through the streets. Cycling to Downtown, Josh swerved between potholes. He skidded through the puddles, weaved in and out of cars, the water splashing around his legs and spraying up from his wheels. Soon, he was so wet he might as well have jumped in a puddle himself.

Arriving in Downtown, he squinted up at the glass buildings, their shiny surfaces reflecting the water in the streets, blinding him momentarily. Way above him, the freeway curled through the skyscrapers like a monorail floating through the air. He took a turn off and, as he entered the forest of skyscrapers, it grew darker and cooler, the buildings starving the streets of light. The towers loomed above him in a spectral way, like enormous prehistoric trees.

The office was in a glass building, dwarfed by the other skyscrapers that stood around it. Josh pushed through the revolving door into the ground floor reception, then took the elevator up to the fifteenth floor.

Walking along the corridor, he saw the fountain; a statue of a man with a beard and wings, a small spout of water streaming from his mouth. Outside the door to Suite 1500, he stopped to check his watch. It was two on the dot. He knocked. Silence. Then the sound of footsteps, and the door opened.

A young woman, in her early 20s, stood on the other side. She was slim, and wore a white blouse and a black skirt. Her hair was cut short in an asymmetric style, her finger nails painted bright pink and she had henna tattoos on her lower arms. She tilted her head to one side and looked Josh up and down.

"Did you swim here?"

"Might as well have done."

"Well, come on in Josh. I'm Daria."

Josh went in delicately, trying not to drip water everywhere.

"Can I take that?" Daria said, looking down at his cycling

helmet.

Josh passed it to her and she took it, holding it carefully like it was some kind of archaeological artifact.

"It's a cycling helmet," he said, feeling he ought to explain. "I came by bike."

"Oh, right. Where from?"

"Brentwood."

"Brentwood?" She raised her eyebrows, looking him over. "You must have very strong legs." She looked around for somewhere to put the helmet, then laid it gently down on a couch.

"Do you need to get changed?"

"That would be great."

"The bathroom's down the hall. And can I get you something to drink?"

"Some water would be nice."

Josh made a hasty change in the bathroom, shoving his wet cycling clothes into his bag. He returned to the lobby, sank into the large black leather couch and picked up the glass of water that was waiting for him.

"Fred will be with you in a moment," Daria said, sitting perched at her computer.

Josh sat back on the couch and looked around the office. It had the air of a travel agency from the 1980s. The walls were decorated with old posters, edges crinkling and turning inwards, the colors faded. There were pictures of ancient rock carvings with elegant figures sculpted into them and snow-covered mountains against bright-blue skies. But the blue had faded to a dull turquoise and the green of the grassy hills had faded to a bleached yellow. There was another poster of a nightclub; people with mullet hairstyles, long sideburns, and thick-rimmed glasses, danced and posed with cocktails. Underneath, it said in thick, black letters: *Tehran, Paris of the Middle East.*

Josh sat looking at the posters. Then, further down the corridor, he noticed a door that was slightly open. He could just hear the sound of a man's voice on a telephone coming from inside. He strained his ears to hear the conversation.

"So what if he doesn't want a big palace? We build him a

small one." Brief silence. "What do you mean they can't do it? Are you *divuneh*? Look you're starting to bug me. If he wants to do business, great. If not, he can *boro gom sho*." The phone slammed down. "Damn foreigners!"

Daria walked down the corridor. She knocked twice on the door, then entered. A few moments later, she came out again, and returned to Josh on the couch.

"Fred can see you now. He just had a *slightly* stressful conversation, but I think he's recovered."

Josh got up and walked down the corridor. When he got to the door, he knocked twice, gently.

"Come in," said a voice inside.

Josh pushed the door and went in.

Inside, it was gloomy, and Josh's eyes struggled to adjust to the light. The blinds were down but half-open and just enough sunlight streamed in to illuminate the room. The air was heavy, the furniture covered with a thick layer of dust. In the middle stood a large table and, all around, piles of papers were stacked on the floor. Beneath them was the occasional glimpse of carpet, frayed and stained. An old, limp flag in green, white and red hung on the wall. Underneath the flag was a framed, giant-sized one dollar bill.

On the far side of the room, a man stood looking out the window. He was short, and wore black suit trousers and a white shirt with a tie. His top button was undone, as if he had just ripped it open in order to ventilate. He had a short, stubbly beard and thick-lensed glasses. Josh noticed he wasn't wearing any shoes; his black scraggly socks, too big for him, hung loosely on his feet. At the far edge of the room, a door stood open, leading into a small bathroom; through the door sat a small pair of plastic sandals.

As Josh walked in, Fred turned to face him. He looked at Josh for a moment without saying anything, then gestured vaguely around the room.

"Take a seat."

Josh pulled up a chair and sat down. It was an office chair with wheels, but still in the plastic covering. He looked out across the table. The entire surface was covered with papers and empty coffee cups, like a tidal wave had swept through, deposited several years of office clutter, then passed on.

Fred left the window, walked round to the other side of the table, and sat down. He began to clear away some of the mess but gave up after a few seconds, leaning back in his chair, settling his gaze on Josh.

"You brought a resume?"

"Yes." Josh took a single page of crisp paper out of a blue plastic wallet and passed it over. Fred leaned forward to take it, then settled back in his chair and began to read. He studied the paper hard, as if deciphering what it said. Occasionally, he glanced up at Josh, and then back down at the paper, as if checking that the person in front of him was the same person he was reading about. After a minute, he looked up and pointed to the top of the page.

"It says here you went to Harvard."

"Yes."

"You sure it was Harvard?"

"Yes, it was definitely Harvard."

Fred raised his eyebrows and looked at Josh as if he didn't completely believe him, but couldn't be bothered to argue. He continued reading. A few moments later, he looked up again.

"You're American?"

"Yes..."

"*Fully* American?"

"Fully American."

He continued reading, then he put the paper down, and looked at Josh.

"American," he said slowly. He sighed. "You see, the thing about Americans is..." He paused to look at Josh. "Rich in possessions, but very young souls."

He sat quietly, looking at Josh.

"You know, America would be nothing without us. This country was built on the money from our oil." He paused. "The *CIA*. It was all because of the *CIA*. They'd been watching us. You ever heard of the *300 Committee*? *The Club of Rome*? They were controlling Iran. For years. They were secretly running the country."

He fell silent and looked across the room. He sat, thinking to himself. There was a long pause.

"I'll tell you something else." He leaned forward across the table. "I'm reading a book at the moment. It explains how everything–everything–came from Iran. It's very important. Take anything in the world, anything… I'll tell you how it came from Iran."

Josh wasn't sure if it was his turn to speak. He waited for Fred to continue.

"I mean it. You name something, I'll show you it came from Iran."

He looked at Josh expectantly. "Go on. Anything."

Josh looked around the room. "Air-conditioning," he said.

"Yes! Good one. This came from Iran. The *yakhchal*… used for storing ice and food in the hot desert. Try another."

Josh tried to think of things that had been on his mind all day. Beer. He'd been craving a beer all day.

"OK, what about beer?"

"Yes, again! Beer… this is coming from the Zagros Mountains in Iran. 5000 years ago. I saw it in a museum."

Josh wasn't sure if Fred was making this up. He was doing a good job if he was.

He looked around the room, searching for one more thing. There was a poster of rock carvings with someone carrying a spear.

"OK… how about Britney Spears?"

"Another one! Actually the spear is coming from Iran–"

At that moment, Daria arrived at the door.

"Josh, you forgot your water."

She came in and handed it to Josh. He thanked her and she left.

There was a pause as Fred sat, smiling. Then he placed the resume on the desk, picked up a pen, and began making notes on it. Josh listened to the nib scratching the paper. Fred continued writing for a couple of minutes. When he finished, he clicked the lid back on the pen, put it down, and looked up at Josh.

"So, Mr. Mayhew. As you know, this is a real estate business. We're one of the leading firms in the field. We have built for ourselves here a very fine and expert business, and I have great visions for LA. We are going to transform it. This city might not like Persian architecture, but they will by the time I've finished with it."

Josh nodded.

"Now, you may be wondering about our name, *Telikani-Rezvani*. Why the name? When I started out, it was just me, but I didn't want people to know that. *Hello, it's Fred Latifi from Latifi Real Estate*. It doesn't sound good. But if I say, it's Fred Latifi from *Telikani-Rezvani Real Estate*, well, there's me, there's Mr. Telikani, and there's Mr. Rezvani. Three people, not one. You see what I'm getting at?"

Josh continued to nod.

"Anyway, it's a good business we have made for ourselves. Very good. And right now, we are going through a period of expansion. I have ambitions, and for that, I need help."

"Now. I look at you. I look at your resume. And I think to myself: this could be someone we need. You're educated. You're bright. You have a good appearance. You seem to have good social skills."

"Thank you."

"You could be just the type of person we need."

"Well, great," Josh said.

"But there's a problem."

"What's that?"

Fred leaned forward, looking at Josh intently. His voice reduced almost to a whisper. "Local people," he said, "they don't trust us. They talk about the 'Canadians'. The Canadians have done this, the Canadians have done that."

"The Canadians?"

"We know who they mean," he said, voice raised to normal now. "We know who they're talking about. Us! The Persians!"

"I see…"

"So, what we need is someone people trust. They don't trust us. But you're American. So people will trust you."

"Right."

"Yes. And so, I think to myself, maybe this is the type of man we want."

"Well, I'm hard-working, I'd be happy to turn my hand to most things."

"In that case," Fred said, standing up, a beaming smile across his face, "the answer is yes. Congratulations, Mr. Mayhew, you've got yourself a job." He held his hand out for Josh to shake.

They shook hands firmly. "Right," Fred said, pushing his chair back. "I think now it's time to get back to work." He walked round from behind his desk and headed over to the door. Josh took this as his prompt to do the same.

Back down the corridor, they arrived where Daria was sitting at her computer, blowing her finger nails as more pink paint dried on them.

"Daria, make up a badge for Josh. We have a new addition to the team."

Daria smiled at him and Josh returned it. Fred was just turning to leave, but he noticed Josh smiling as he did so.

"Oh, Josh, one more thing." He beckoned to him. Josh followed him a little way down the corridor.

"Just a small thing. If I ever hear that you've been misbehaving with a Persian woman, or talking with a Persian woman, or even just *looking* at a Persian woman then... how do you Americans say? *Your ass won't be worth a single lousy dime.* Is that clear?"

The remark came so out of the blue that Josh was momentarily stunned.

"Is that clear?"

"Yes," he said. "That's absolutely fine."

"Good," Fred said, giving him a warm beaming smile. "I'm glad we've got that straight. Well, it was a pleasure meeting you. Daria will show you out. And now, if you don't mind, I have business I must attend to."

Fred guided Josh back towards the lobby.

"Daria," he said, "would you mind showing Josh the way out?"

"Sure," Daria said, putting down her nail brush and coming out from behind her computer.

She smiled at Josh and opened the door for him.

"Khoda hafez!" Fred called from down the corridor.

Chapter 20

The following Monday, Josh set out for his first proper day of work. And thus began his new daily gauntlet of swerving through traffic along Wilshire Boulevard, dodging honking cars and angry-faced drivers shouting abuse at him. He arrived in Downtown sweaty but, as he would do each day from now on, relieved. And, as would become routine, Daria answered the office door.

"Hi Josh," she said, takeaway coffee cup in her hand. "We're just sitting down for our weekly meeting. Come through–you can meet the team."

She led him through to a meeting room where several people were seated around a big glass table. Josh exchanged smiles with everyone then sat down.

"So," Daria said, "why don't we start off with introductions? Josh, meet the *Telikani-Rezvani Real Estate* team. First, there's me, Daria. I sit at the front and answer the phone. I like to think of myself as the public face of the operation. Whatever gets thrown in our direction–whining lawyers, complaining developers–I am the first buffer. So, if you have any queries, I should be your first port of call. Now, to the left here, we have Firuzeh."

Firuzeh was large, cheerful, and had an expansive chest. She was a Mother Earth figure, with big friendly cheeks and lots of wobbling flesh. When she smiled, her whole face crinkled up.

"Firuzeh does our accounts."

"Och," she said, pinching Josh's cheek. "Fred told me *all* about you."

"Salaam," Josh said.

"Ooch," Firuzeh said. "He speaks Persian!" She squeezed his cheek again, and tweaked other bits of him: arm, stomach, and then his cheek a final time. "*Che khoshteep*!"

"That means cute," Daria said, looking embarrassed. "Right, so that's Firuzeh. By the way, Firuzeh means *Woman of Triumph*. Fred hired her to bring good luck to the business. And then," she said, turning to her right, "this is Arash. He's our tech wizard."

Arash wore baggy jeans that hung around his thighs and bright red sneakers, the laces undone. His hair was thickly gelled into a black quiff, with streaks shaved off along the sides. Around his neck, he wore a gold chain, and there were tattoos on his lower arms. A pair of massive headphones, like halved coconuts, hung around his neck, as if he'd just played a set.

He gave a silent upward nod of the head. "It's not my field or anything," he said. "I'm just doing it before going to dental school." He fell silent and looked glum.

"And that's the team," Daria said.

"And Fred?" Josh said.

"Just on his way."

Then, with perfect timing, Fred marched through the door, walking quickly and looked flustered. He was wearing the same tired suit that hung limply around his body. He sat down and shuffled his papers. Everyone else sprang into action, sitting up to attention.

"Khub," said Fred. "Are we all here?" He looked around the table. "You've all had a chance to meet Josh?"

There was a general murmur of 'yes'.

"Josh is the latest member of *T-R Associates*. He comes to us with a distinguished record in the real estate business. He will be an accomplished member of the team."

He paused, frowning.

"I must say, if I could have my way, I would conduct our meetings in Persian. Speaking English… it pains my heart. My father, he is an educated man. But he refuses. I have no choice. In the modern world of real estate, English is necessary."

There was a slightly awkward pause.

"But, moving on. Daria, please–the agenda this week."

Daria looked down at her notes. "Well, first," she said, "the new multi-family apartments in Studio City are selling well. Just three to go and then we're done."

"Good. Well done. Next?"

"Next… the replica White House on Lower Mulholland."

"How's that coming along?"

"Well he's fine with it being one-third of the size. But he now wants a replica Oval Office in the East Wing."

"I thought we discussed–"

"He's pretty adamant about it."

"OK, OK, I'll see what I can do. Right, next: how about that building on Rodeo?"

"Yes, Arash met with him the other day."

"It's coming along," said Arash.

"Remember," Fred said, "Mr. Ahmadi wants blue carpet and gold curtain rods."

"OK…"

"Not the other way around."

"Hey," Arash said, lifting his hands up with the palms out.

"And he wants his home cinema to seat *100* people. Not 50."

"A hundred?"

"Yes."

"Does he *know* 100 people?"

"Probably not, but it doesn't matter. He's an old friend from high school in Tehran. I want him to be happy."

"Right," Daria said. "That's all on my list. Anyone got anything else?"

"Well," Arash said, "next month, we're due to build our 1000th column."

"You serious?" Fred said.

"Yes."

"That's fantastic. Let's throw a party. Firuzeh–make that happen."

Firuzeh nodded and made a note.

Arash continued. "And, one thing I heard: Beverly Hills council have launched new complaints about the Mahjoub residence on Canon Drive."

"Eh?"

"It was reported in the *Weekly* yesterday." He picked up a newspaper clipping. "Squatting astride Canon Drive," he read, "the size of an iceberg and as gaudy as a wedding cake, the latest Persian monstrosity makes the Taj Mahal look like a child's Lego set."

"Tell 'em to get lost…" Fred said.

"… strong enough to withstand a grade nine earthquake, the

structure has riled local residents for damaging the fabric of the city and destroying buildings of historic interest…"

"Historic interest?"

"That's what it says."

"*Historic interest*? They're telling me those piles of rubbish are historic interest?"

"Well," Arash said, checking through the article, "yes… that's the term they use."

"History? They can't talk to *us* about history. We're Persian. We know about history. We've got *four thousand years* of history in Iran."

"I know… I know," said Arash.

"I mean, I tell you. You take anything… anything… and I show you it comes from Iran. Come on, try me…"

"Yes, OK Fred…"

"Alright, alright," Fred said, calming down now. "Don't worry. I'll deal with them. Right, any other business?"

"I wanted to mention," Firuzeh said tentatively, "the handicapped signs in your car."

"What do you mean?"

"Someone's complained that perhaps—"

"But I *am* handicapped…"

"Yes, but the problem is, you're doing it, your cousins down the block are doing it… it's starting to look suspicious. Not *everyone* can be handicapped…"

"OK, OK, I'll think about it. Arash, how's the website going?"

"Well," he said slowly, chewing over his words, "there are still a few problems…"

"You know I don't understand the website," Fred said. "I leave that to you. Daria—what about the statue in Downtown?"

"Still waiting on planning permission."

"OK. Just tell them they need a statue of *Cyrus the Great*. Downtown can't be Downtown without it."

"There was opposition from the Kurdish community. They said Cyrus was Kurdish, not Persian…"

"Tell them to get lost. Everyone knows Kurds are just mountain Iranians. And the Americans—they should be grateful. Thomas Jefferson based the US constitution on Cyrus' cylinder.

It was in *National Geographic*…"

At that moment, Fred's phone went off. He picked it up and looked confused, trying to figure out what to press. He hit a few buttons hopefully. "Allo? No. No. Allo?" Arash leant over to help, but Fred had had enough. He jabbed his finger at the screen and the phone went dead.

Fred shuffled his papers and paused to make a couple of notes. Then he looked up. "Good," he said, "so, I think that brings things to a close. We can resume discussions tomorrow. For today–" He stopped mid-sentence. He was looking straight across the room. His gaze was cast in the direction of Daria.

Daria had been going through her papers, but now she looked up and noticed Fred staring at her.

"Something wrong?" she said.

There was a pause.

"Daria," Fred said, "what's that?"

"What?"

"That," he said, pointing at her face.

Daria moved her hand up to her face. She held it over her nose for a moment, then she paused, like she had found something. She held it there self-consciously.

"Nothing."

"I'm sorry?"

"I said it's nothing."

"Doesn't look like nothing to me."

Pause.

"It's a nose stud," she said quietly under her breath.

Fred looked at her. Another pause. "Louder please?"

"A nose stud."

There was silence. Fred looked at her, his expression blank. Josh hadn't noticed, but now, if he looked closely, he could see a very small, silver stud in the dip of Daria's nose. Barely visible, only when it caught the light and reflected it in a tiny dash of silver was it noticeable.

"Daria, would you like to explain why there's some silver in your nose?"

"It's a nose stud. I got it done for my birthday."

Fred sat motionless looking at her. "Do your parents know

about this?"

"No."

"Do they know you have a lump of metal in your nose?"

"Fred..." Firuzeh said.

"Do they know your face is covered in *junk*?"

Arash shuffled uncomfortably in his chair. Josh stared at his papers and tried not to get involved.

"Fred..." Firuzeh said again.

"Do they know you are walking around like some kind of hooker who–"

"*Fred...*"

"–who's just come in off the street? Bringing shame on your grandparents? After all your family have done for you, giving you a good life in this country, and you choose to dress like that..."

"Oh, for God's sake!" said Daria, shoving her papers across the table, pushing back her chair and standing up.

"Now, come on, Daria," Firuzeh said.

"I'm sorry. This is *ridiculous*. I come in one day with a *tiny* nose stud and you start to complain. I can't believe–"

"I'm not complaining," Fred said. "I'm simply saying–"

"No, I don't want to hear it. This is *typical*. One tiny, little thing that you don't approve of and–"

"*Daria...*"

"I don't care. I've had enough. It's stupid. If I was a guy, I'd be able to do whatever I want. Arash is some kind of *doodool tala*. Just because I'm a *girl*..."

Arash glanced up with a '*hey, that's a bit harsh*' expression.

"It's always the same. The guys get to do what they want and the girls have to follow orders. It's unfair and... and... *medieval*."

She shoved her chair behind her.

"And anyway," she said, "my grandparents are back in Iran, so that's sort of irrelevant, isn't it?"

She stormed out of the room, slamming the door on the way. A deep silence descended. Josh sat still and wasn't sure where to direct his eyes. Eventually, he decided to just focus on a point somewhere around the middle of the table.

"*Doodool tala*," Firuzeh whispered to him. "Golden penis."

Fred cleared his throat, then looked back down at his papers. There was a long pause.

"Fred," Firuzeh said turning to him. "You shouldn't–"

"Firuzeh. I'd prefer it if you stayed out of this."

"But she's just a girl–"

"*Exactly*. She's just a girl. She's no business going around with metal in her nose."

"But–"

"Enough," Fred said. "This is my office and there is no place here for young women with pieces of metal in their nose."

There was an awkward pause. Josh continued looking down at the table. Arash did the same. Fred shuffled his papers. There were a few moments of silence.

"The thing is," he said, "it's not *khanom*-like. You know? Iranian girls going around with bits of metal in their noses will not grow up to be decent young women. Maybe I am old-fashioned, but it's just not how girls should behave."

There was a short silence, everyone reluctant to fill it. Finally Fred spoke again.

"When I grew up, you know what I was called? *Son of Yahya.* That was my name. People knew. They knew I was the son of someone and I had to respect my parents because of that. But over here? Here, young people do whatever they want. It's not proper."

There was another pause. Firuzeh was about to say something, but she thought better of it. Everyone looked back down at their papers.

"Right," Fred said. "Unless there is anything else, I think we can call the meeting closed."

Chapter 21

The next few weeks were glorious. Josh cycled to work, cruising along Wilshire Boulevard each morning. Of course, he still had to dodge the buses and the occasional rain shower meant he got soaked, but he was so relieved to have a job, it didn't matter whether he arrived at work looking like he had swum there.

For the first time in a long while, he felt like he actually had some purpose in life. Rather than just cycling aimlessly around the city, at last he had something to *do* each day. Sure, it wasn't the classic Californian lifestyle he'd imagined. He didn't stroll cheerily down his garden path each morning, saying *hi* to his neighbor as they watered their lawn. He didn't drive to work listening to the morning talk radio, or rather, in the case of LA, listening to the traffic reports while sitting in perpetual sun-drenched gridlock. But it was a sort of scaled down version of that, California 'lite', with a bike instead of a car. And anyway, he thought, he wouldn't *want* to be stuck in a car. He looked at all the commuters in their vehicles; sooner or later they'd suffer the same fate as the guy in that movie–they'd jump out of their cars, hurl their croissants and lattes across the freeway, and go on some kind of rampage across the city. On a bike, however, he was sane. On a bike, he was safe.

At the same time, there was another change coming. Spring was in the air. The rains of January had passed and the weather was finally warming up. Flowers were blooming. Blossom littered the sidewalks. Along the coast, pink bodies with pale wintery flesh appeared on the beaches and a few adventurous souls dipped themselves in the water.

In the office, spring had arrived as well. Computer mice sat still as people gazed out of office windows. Everyone longed to be outside. There was an unspoken recognition that work had been temporarily put aside. Firuzeh buzzed around the office like a kindly bee, stopping to deliver dried fruit and nuts to the staff, and in-between times, preparing big plastic tubs of soup destined for the street kitchens of Skid Row.

"You know, Josh, I've been thinking," she said one day. "You need to find yourself a girlfriend."

"We've already talked about this Firuzeh…"

"No, a *Persian* girlfriend."

Arash looked up. He was sitting behind his computer. Today, his jeans were weighed down with a gold-studded belt so heavy he had to hold onto the sides to keep them up.

"Last thing you should do," he said. "Trust me. Persian girls? Nothing but trouble."

"Oh, come, Arash, no need for that," Firuzeh said.

"I've been there. Nothing but trouble."

"If he wants a Persian girlfriend, let him," Firuzeh said. "He can decide for himself."

"Well, I don't recommend it."

"That's just your experience."

"It's a fact, universally acknowledged…" began Arash, then he fell quiet as Fred passed by the door.

"Look," Firuzeh whispered, Fred out of earshot now. "If you're interested in someone, just tell me. I'll know her mother. I can introduce you." Josh mouthed a *thank you* and swung back on his chair.

As well as distributing food, Firuzeh had been decorating the office. Bouquets of fuchsia and violets stood in vases. In the kitchen, there were little plates of bite-sized walnut cookies flavored with cardamom and honey, and on the window sill stood a glass bowl containing goldfish.

"Firuzeh," Josh said, "what's with all the office decorations?"

She looked surprised. "Don't you know? They're for Nowruz."

"No what?"

"Nowruz. New Year."

"New Year? But that's in December."

"For you, yes. Not for us. Persian New Year is in spring."

"And that's because…?"

"It's when everything comes to life. That truly is the start of a new year. For nature."

Josh nodded in understanding.

"So," Firuzeh said, "how will you celebrate?"

"I haven't planned anything."

"No plans?" she said, a look of genuine horror on her face. "But, you must have plans. In Iran, we say a person who does not celebrate New Year is like… well… it is unthinkable. Arash, joon, how can we help Josh? It's Nowruz and he doesn't have anything to do."

Arash looked up wearily from his computer. "You can join us if you like. We're heading down to Manhattan Beach tonight. Come along."

"Josh," Firuzeh said, looking at him solemnly, "you should definitely go."

***

That evening, Josh cycled down to Arash's apartment in Culver City. The days were getting longer now, and the dusky evening light cast a pastel glow over the city.

Arash greeted him at the door of his apartment as he arrived.

"Josh! What's up? You got here just in the nick of time. We're ready to roll boy. Get ya jacket and let's hit the road."

Josh locked up his bike while Arash and his mates emerged from the house. Like Arash, their jeans hung around their lower hips, bits of dangly metal jewelry clinking and clanging.

"This is Kourosh," Arash said, "currently at Law School. Siavash, currently pre-med. And Mahmoud, electrical engineering. But we don't talk to him," he said, smiling and punching him on the arm, "he's an 818 kid."

"Sorry, what?" Josh asked, confused.

"An 818 kid. The area code, 818."

As they piled into Arash's car, it creaked and sank several inches lower. It was kitted out with a low-slung chassis, spoilers, black-tinted windows, and an exhaust so heavy it looked like it would drag along the floor. Rap music rumbled through the speakers and the car trembled with the bass. They crawled menacingly through the night like a shark prowling the ocean floor.

As they cruised south, the city lights faded into black behind them. Along the streets hung banners and flags advertising

137

Persian New Year. The coast opened up away to their right.

Down at the beach, people had parked their cars in an area just off the road. The sand sprayed out beneath the wheels as they skidded to a halt. As they climbed out of the car, the ocean breeze was cool against the skin.

They started to walk down towards the sea, their footsteps growing heavy across the sand. Further down the beach, groups of people sat on rugs, clustered around portable cauldrons of bubbling soup and makeshift barbecues. Further away, he could see people building a bonfire out of bits of wood, old clothes and ripped up cardboard boxes. It tapered up to about his own height, looming in the darkness like some kind of ragged pagoda.

"That's the bonfire," Arash said. "For Chaharshanbe Suri."

A girl who had been building it stood back to admire her work, dusting the sand off her hands. A few people cleared the area around the bonfire, kicking away stray bits of debris. Then a man picked up some petrol, unscrewed the lid, and, heaving the can with both hands, doused the bonfire with a few splashes. He pulled out some matches from the back pocket of his jeans and scraped one against the box. A brief spark of light appeared in the dark, then the match flickered into life. He held it aloft for a moment, the flame wavering and spluttering, then he threw it onto the bonfire. There was a moment while it took light, then an orange flame streaked its way around the pyramid, and the bonfire burst into life.

The fire threw flickering light onto the shadowy silhouetted figures on the beach. But soon it had spent its energy. From inside the pyramid of junk, there was a creaking noise, and a moment later, it sighed and collapsed, disintegrating in a smoldering heap. The flames began to subside and soon it was just a pile of glowing red ash with the occasional flickering flame.

"And now," Arash said, turning to Josh, "the fun begins."

Everyone got up and formed two lines leading up to the bonfire. One man walked in-between the lines, up to the fire. He got to the edge and stopped, looking out over the smoldering orange ash. He turned to the people lined up.

"May this fire take our sickness and our problems, and replace them with warmth and energy."

He turned around to face the fire once more, then walked back several paces. Then, like a long-jumper, he ran, with gathering speed, towards the fire. When he reached the edge, he leapt, sailing over the heap of burning ash and rubble, landing beyond, and rolling onto his side in the sand. Everyone cheered and clapped, and the jumper turned back to the fire and saluted the flames.

Now it was the others' turn. The next person took their run up and leapt over the bonfire. They only just made it, flying through the dark and thumping into the sand just beyond the glowing embers on the other side. The jumpers continued, each taking their turn. Each time someone ran and jumped, there was a crescendo of noise, and a cheer, as they passed over the bonfire.

Josh hung back until the end. When his turn came, he took a step back to brace himself for the leap, then he sprinted as fast as he could, and, at the edge of the bonfire, leapt high and far. For a moment, he felt himself pass through a body of warm air, then the air felt cool again, then he felt the heavy thud of the sand. He rolled over in the dark. A cheer rose up from the crowd.

Everyone had jumped now; the crowd began to disperse. Slowly, people began to regroup and sit down in clusters around the bonfire, cross-legged on the sand. The ashes still burned, sending out a steady orange glow. Then somewhere, someone took out a guitar. The sound of gently strummed chords and singing drifted across the beach.

Josh turned to the person sitting behind him. "What do the words mean?" he said.

"It means: *my butterfly... my butterfly... what can I do without you...*"

He looked back at the person. He couldn't see much of her in the darkness, just a shadowy figure in the gloom.

"You know what it's about?" she said.

"No."

"It's a love song. It's about unrequited love."

There was a moment's silence.

"I'm Sepideh," she said, holding out her hand. Josh took it and they shook. He looked at her again through the darkness. He could make out her clothes now: black jeans and a black leather jacket. For a moment the fire cast a flickering light on her face and he could make out her features: dark eyes, thin face and lips, thin eyebrows, deep-brown skin, and long, dark hair.

"Well," he said, suddenly feeling a little uncomfortable in the silence. "That was quite a display."

"You've never been to a Chaharshanbe Suri before?"

"I'd never heard of it until today."

"Ah. So I guess you're not Iranian?"

"No."

Another slight pause as they fell into silence.

"But you know the meaning of it?" Sepideh said.

"Something about Nowruz…"

"It's about getting ready for the New Year. Purifying yourself before the arrival of spring."

There was another pause as Josh tried to think of something intelligent to say.

"It kind of reminds me of that song," he said eventually.

"Which one?"

"You know… that song… by… thingy…"

"No."

"You know, the one that goes… er…"

"You'll have to sing it for me."

"You know… *The Power of Love*… or something."

"Nope, don't know it."

"Come on. 'Course you do. It's been everywhere."

"Sing it for me…"

He cleared his throat. "*Duh duh duh duh duuuh duh…*" he sang, "*… something something…* I can't remember the words."

"Doesn't ring any bells," she said, pretending to give it some thought. "Sing some more."

Josh sighed. "Come on, you must know it."

"No…"

"Anyway, I'm a crap singer."

"Doesn't matter…"

"And you'll never get it anyway…"

"But I thought you just said everyone knew it…"

"Yeah… I know… but now I'm not so sure."

She sat back on the sand. In the gloom, he could just see her putting on a pretend sulky face.

"OK," he said. He cleared his throat again. "*The Power of Love,*" he said tentatively, throat slightly creaky. "*Duh duh duh duh….I can't re-meeeem-ber…*" He stopped. Sepideh seemed to be shaking.

"What?"

Through the gloom, he could see she was trembling silently.

"What is it?" She was bent over now, struggling to get her words out. "Is there something wrong?"

"That is just… I can't quite describe–"

"OK, whatever…"

"I honestly can say–"

"That was actually quite a good rendition," Josh said, sticking up for himself.

She tried to regain her composure. "I'm sorry. It's rude to laugh at someone you've only just met."

"You don't say…"

"And especially when they're trying to sing…"

"Trying?"

"When they *are* singing. Beautifully. And, let's admit, it's difficult to find beauty in an '80s power ballad."

"Hey, watch what you say! '80s power ballads sustained me through my youth."

"OK, I guess we'll just have to disagree on that one. Anyway," she said, regaining her composure, "I think the message is slightly different."

"How?"

"Well that was about love… purging your soul. Nowruz is more about… well, just the fire."

"OK. But… similar."

"Yeah, similar, I guess."

They fell silent. There was just the sound of the embers burning on the fire, and the murmur of other conversations drifting over the sand.

"So, who did you come here with?" Josh asked.

"My sister. She's over there," she said, nodding across the sand. "Yourself?"

"Just some friends." He pointed over towards Arash.

"Oh. The Persian gangsters. I wondered who they were."

"I work with one of them." There was a brief silence. "So," said Josh, feeling that she had gotten the better of him in the conversation so far. "What are two beautiful women like you and your sister doing out by yourselves?"

"Oh, nothing much." She paused for a moment. "Anyway, that's very forward."

"What?"

"Calling us beautiful. And a bit presumptuous, that we're out alone."

"I didn't presume..."

"You did. You said *what are two beautiful women like you and your sister doing out alone.*"

"Right, well, when I said alone I meant–"

"I'm pretty offended that you should just jump to that conclusion..."

"Hey, come on..."

"It's pretty arrogant, if you ask me..."

"Look, I really didn't mean anything–"

"Downright audacious, one might say..."

She turned away in a huff.

"Look," Josh said. "I'm sorry. It was just a throw-away remark."

"You'll have to try harder than that."

"OK, I'm really sorry."

"Harder."

"I'm desperately, truly, agonizingly sorry..."

"That's better."

She turned back to face him. He saw her face again in the dark now. She had thin, frail features, almost snake-like.

He thought he'd try again. "So," he said. "You didn't answer my question."

"I guess we're just out alone, searching for what the future might deliver."

"Right. And that could be..."

"That could be... anything." She smiled an enigmatic smile. "So," she said, "how are you going to make it up to me?"

"What do you mean?"

"For your earlier offense. I think it's only right that you should make amends."

"I thought I'd got away with that."

"Almost, but I haven't quite forgotten."

"I guess... I could just say I'm sorry?"

"Hhmm, good start. But I think it'll take a little more than that."

"Well, you tell me what I could do."

"I think taking me out for a meal would be sufficient."

Josh smiled. "I can do that."

"Well," she said, "in that case, we had better swap numbers."

He took out his phone and began typing as she read it out. She peered over his shoulder to check he got it correct.

"OK," she said. "That's that, then. I guess we'll be in touch. Right?"

"Right."

There was a moment's silence. They just sat looking at each other. "Well," she said. "It's probably time I rejoined my sister. It was nice meeting you."

"Nice to meet you, too."

She looked at him, subtly trying to grab a last glance at his face in the gloom. Then she smiled, hoisted herself up, and dusted the sand off the front of her jeans.

"Bye," she said, smiling down at him, with a little wave.

"Bye," he said, looking up at her.

Then she turned and walked away from the dim light of the fire, into the black shadows beyond.

Chapter 22

At his desk the following morning, Josh stared at the screen. His mind was preoccupied with the night before: the bonfire on the beach, the leaping over the fire, the music, and Sepideh.

He took his shoes off and, finding sand in them, emptied it into the bin. He checked to see if Sepideh's number was actually in his phone and, yes, it was. His mind wandered back to their conversation and what she looked like. It was so dark, he hadn't been able to see her properly. All he had in his mind was the hazy image of her shadowy face in the half-light of the beach.

Arash passed by the door.

"Good time last night?"

"Great. Thanks for inviting me."

"Nice to have you along. By the way, who was that girl you were talking to?"

"Oh, I don't know. Just some random person."

"I think she might have been Mahmoud's cousin. Remember, 818 area codes. You've been warned…"

Josh picked up his phone again and started writing a text.

Sepideh, nice to meet you last night. Even though you laughed at my singing. Let's meet again sometime. J

He put down the phone and turned back to his computer. The spreadsheet on the multi-family property in North Hollywood was even less exciting than it had looked the previous day. Fortunately, he didn't have to wait long before a distraction arrived. His phone bleeped a reply.

Nice to meet you too. Sorry for laughing at you. Promise not to do it again. What you doin' tonight? You could come over to my gallery in Venice.

He typed back. *OK. Let me know where. Finish work at 6. Be there by 8.*

He hesitated, wondering whether he should put a kiss. He tried it with one. It looked OK. But then, upon reflection, maybe it was too keen. He deleted it. But now it looked a bit cold. Stuff it, he thought. He put the kiss back in, and one more for good measure.

He hit send, then swung back on his chair, just in time to catch sight of Fred emerging from his office.

"We're almost on our 1000th column. Almost!"

***

The clock changed to six, and Josh was out the office door like a greyhound. He cycled at speed along Wilshire Boulevard, hunched over like an athlete, pedaling long and hard, blasting through the lights just as each one turned red. Back home, he took his fastest ever shower, scrubbing his hair like he was fighting head lice, then tugged on his clothes, like an actor making a speedy scene change.

Then, he was back onto his bike, coasting down the hills towards Santa Monica. He'd been wondering what to bring. Realistically, there was only one option: an enormous bouquet of flowers. He visualized his arrival like the moment in *Pretty Woman* where Richard Gere appears outside the hotel, standing out of the sun roof of his white limousine. Of course, he would be on a bicycle, not in a limousine. But still, he felt it would work.

Stopping at a florist's shop, he bought a bouquet of lilies, then cycled on into Venice, carrying them tucked carefully under one arm. Arriving at Vernon Avenue, he paused, then a little further down, he saw what he was aiming for: *Zahedi Fine Arts Gallery*. It was a small shop, roughly painted in a pastel turquoise.

He locked his bike up against a lamppost. Walking towards the gallery, he smoothed his hair to get rid of the imprints of his helmet. At the door, he looked for a bell, but finding none, gave two hard knocks. The door was wooden, and made a light, hollow sound. As he waited, he rearranged the flowers in the bouquet.

There was quiet from inside. He peered through the window but the gallery was empty. Then he heard a sound from the back. He saw Sepideh appear through the door. She wore a long, green dress, dark hair flowing around her shoulders. She opened the door, standing back to take him in.

145

"You look like you've just cycled the *Tour de France*."

"I pretty much did. One stage at least."

"I'm not sure whether I can let you in looking like that."

"Well, you might have a dead body on your hands. I'm about to collapse from dehydration."

"That's your fault for not having a car."

"You'd be an accomplice to murder…"

"Oh, OK then. In you come."

Looking at her now in daylight, her skin was a deep bronze, like earthy copper. Her eyes shone like jewels and she had perfect, white teeth. Her thin facial features made her look almost serpent-like, but her eyes glowed with a comforting warmth. Her dark-green dress brought out the deep bronze of her skin.

He handed her the flowers. "A small gift," he said.

"That's bold. Do you always bring flowers the first time you meet someone?"

"No, it's a one-off. Don't know what got into me. Too much Californian sun making me romantic."

"They're very nice. Thank you." She turned and went into the kitchen at the back of the gallery. "I'll get a vase for them."

Josh stepped through the door. It was stark, just a bare concrete floor, with light, white-washed walls. The paintings were mainly large, abstract oils, big bright blotches of color. In the middle of the floor stood a small, blue wooden table with a couple of blue metal foldaway chairs. Sitting down, he put his bag on the floor and listened to Sepideh from the kitchen. He heard her open and close a cupboard, then run water from a tap. She returned carrying the flowers, plumping them in the vase as she walked. She placed them on the table then unfolded one of the chairs and sat down opposite him.

"So," she said, "what have you been up to today?"

"Totally routine. Nonsensical real estate spreadsheets. Nothing out of the ordinary. Oh, except that I got caught gazing into space by my boss, which I blame entirely on you…"

She smiled and smacked his arm. "Apart from that?"

"Apart from that… nothing. You?"

"I sat around in the gallery and tried to sell art."

"Any luck?"

"Nope. One person came in, but he was just a lost tourist trying to get to Hollywood. Not much chance of selling to him."

"Never mind."

"So, in the end, I just started making ice-cream." She picked up a bowl from the table. "Try some."

Josh took a spoon and ate. It was icy on his lips with a delicate, fragrant flavor.

"Saffron rosewater," she said.

They fell silent for a moment.

"I was thinking about what you said the other night," Josh said.

"What?"

"About purging one's soul." He adopted a mock austere expression. "Sepideh, you've purged my heart so completely... I can't imagine ever looking at another woman besides you."

She cringed. "Oh, please," she said, swiping at his arm again. "Listen, I'm just about done here. If you fancy, we could head out and get something to eat."

"Sure. Where?"

"There's a nice little Caribbean place nearby."

She pushed her chair back, scraping on the concrete floor. She went into the kitchen, locked up the back, and closed the shutters on the windows. Josh picked his bag up off the floor. A few moments later, she reappeared.

"All set?"

They passed through the front door. He stood and waited as she locked up, then they set off walking through the quiet back streets of Venice.

"How do you find living around here?" he said after a while.

"It's OK. Not quite Venice Italy. But still..."

"The new world version?"

"Exactly. It has its charms. Less touristy. Less museum-like. Actually has real people living in it."

"It's got a neighborhood feel to it."

"I suppose so. But I wouldn't say I feel like a local yet. Then again, I don't think many people here feel like locals. It's hard if you're not born here."

They fell quiet as they arrived at a road crossing. Passing over, on the other side, they saw the cantina–a brightly-painted wooden shack with a yellow canvas awning hanging out the side. Underneath it sat wooden tables painted in pastel blues, greens and reds.

There were just a few other people–mostly young couples–enjoying quiet, mid-week meals. Josh and Sepideh found a table. Looking out towards the beach, they could just hear the sound of waves breaking.

As they sat down, a waiter dressed in cut-off shorts and a T-shirt came to take their order.

"Hey guys. What'll it be?"

They hadn't yet looked at the menu. They each took one and cast an eye over it.

"I'll get a chicken curry," Sepideh said.

"And I'll get… the barbecued fish."

"Any drinks with that?"

Josh looked at Sepideh. "You drinking?"

"I will if you will," she said.

"Let's get a bottle, then. A bottle of house white."

They fell into silence. Sepideh was looking out across the restaurant. She seemed to be gazing at something, her eyes fixed on a point lost in the distance. Then whatever was on her mind washed over her, and she turned to face Josh. Now he could see her face more clearly, he saw she was a little older than he had thought. No wrinkles or anything. It almost wasn't physical. Just a hint of age somehow.

"So," he said. "Have you revised your negative view on power ballads?"

"Well… I've been trying."

"I think you should."

"I guess, on reflection, perhaps they aren't so bad. But only when you're singing them."

"Sounds like you're coming round to the idea."

The food arrived quickly, two plates with steaming white rice, garnished with freshly-washed cilantro, so fragrant it felt healthy just breathing in the fumes. They ate quietly, pausing only to smile at each other from time to time and look out across the beach.

At the end, they put their knives and forks down, napkins on the table, and sat back in their chairs.

Josh looked out over the dusky beach, the sun down now. "Don't you think LA is just wonderful?"

"You serious?"

"Yeah."

"What makes you say that?"

"It's just great. The freedom… the space."

"You're the first person I've heard say that."

"Really?"

"Sure. Most people hate it. A sun-drenched graveyard where you can decay in complete bliss."

"Who said that?" Josh asked.

"Don't know. Anyway, I find it soulless."

"What do you mean? It's got so much soul."

"How long have you been here?" Sepideh said.

"About six months."

"You need to try it a bit longer than that."

"Well, hang on. Let's be realistic," Josh said. "How many places can you use skateboards as a viable means of transportation?"

"Only if you work less than a mile from where you live…"

"Or escape reality by living in a dream world based on movies and TV."

"Well, some people like a slightly firmer grip on real life." She took a sip of her wine. "The thing about LA is… it's got no *oomph*."

"Oomph?"

"Yeah, you know, just… something's missing. That's the only way I can put it. No heart."

She paused before continuing.

"There's this thing in Iran. It's called *safaa*. It's like this bond between people. A sort of warmth. People lock eyes with you, you're safe with them, there's a connection–you're all part of a community. There's nothing like that here. Everyone's a stranger. Everyone's isolated. *Safaa*? It doesn't exist. Even Iranians lose it."

They fell silent for a few moments.

"When did you come here?" Josh said.

"I was fifteen. Been dealing with the whole dual-identity thing ever since."

"What do you mean?"

"You know, growing up in Iran, coming to America."

"Have you been back?"

"Once. I visited our family home. But it was strange. It felt like I'd never been there. When I walked around my neighborhood, I couldn't even recognize any of the buildings. It was all new. It looked like a foreign city."

She paused and took a sip of wine, looking away towards the ocean. She put her glass back down and looked at Josh.

"On one level, it was weird. But on another, it made me realize I didn't have a choice. In terms of being American. It was like a voice said: *you're not Iranian anymore. You can't be. You're American and only American.*"

They fell into silence again.

"Anyway," she said, "enough about me. What about you?"

"I'm not very interesting."

"I don't believe that."

"Grew up in New Jersey. Basically spent my whole life there. I'm American, through and through. About as American as apple pie."

"Come on. The waters must get muddy somewhere."

"Well, I guess I've always been torn over which '80s power ballad–"

Sepideh groaned.

"–is the greatest. I mean, is it Sinead O'Connor, *Nothing Compares to You*? Or Celine Dion, *All Coming Back to Me Now*?"

She clamped her hands over her ears and buried her head on the table.

"OK," he said, "we won't go there. Dessert. What shall it be?"

"I don't think I can handle anything sweet."

"Really?"

"You're sweet enough for me Josh…"

"That was far worse… *far* worse…"

They sat a while longer, absorbing the late evening peace. It was just beginning to get dark. Through the bits of corrugated metal that made up the walls, Josh could see the ocean and the waves lapping at the shore. There were still a few figures on the beach, evening surfers walking home across the sand, boards under their arms.

"Right," she said, breaking him out of his reverie. "Time to go?"

"Sure."

They stood up and thanked the waiter. Josh tried to cover the check, but Sepideh intervened.

"I'm older than you."

"Not by much…"

"OK. Compromise. We go halves."

"If you insist."

They paid the check. He turned to her. "Where do you live?"

"Nearby. Close to the gallery."

"I'll walk you back."

They set off through the streets, walking in silence. The sun had set now, and there was a dusky light. The air was slightly cooler and a light breeze came from the ocean. Cars were starting to illuminate their headlamps in the quiet streets. They turned down a side alley onto a row of white-washed apartment buildings, red rose bushes creeping over white walls and trees heavy with pink cherry blossom.

"OK," Sepideh said, stopping. "This is me."

They were outside a two-story apartment block, a flight of stairs leading up the side to large French doors.

"You know, Josh, I would invite you up, but I don't ordinarily do that on a first date. I hope you understand."

"Of course. No need to apologize."

"But I had a lovely evening. It was nice just… chatting."

They fell into silence again. It didn't feel awkward. They just smiled at each other. Then, as words became unnecessary, they moved closer. He put his hands on her hips, leant forward until his forehead touched hers. They remained that way for a few moments.

"Well," she said, "is this what they mean by a *total eclipse of the heart?*"

Josh laughed. "Not quite. I think she meant something else. But looks like you're learning…"

There was a pause. They each held their position. Their noses were almost touching. He began to tip his head to the side, but she drew away.

She gave him a quick kiss on the cheek, turned around, and skipped lightly up the stairs. When she got to the top, she stopped and turned.

"First dates, Josh. I hope you understand."

Then she turned and disappeared through the French doors.

Josh stood on the sidewalk. He remained for a moment, savoring the warm, still air, then began walking back towards his bike, the scent of cherry blossom all around.

Chapter 23

Two days later, Josh couldn't concentrate at work. Every time he tried to get something done, a thought flitted into his mind, like a moth fluttering into his field of vision. He tried to focus his eyes on the spreadsheet in front of him but the figures blurred and meant nothing.

"We don't pay you to sit and do nothing, Josh."

He looked around. Fred was standing at the doorway.

"Sorry Fred. I was just thinking about that documentation you gave me. It's actually quite–"

"Cut the crap, Josh. We both know there's only one thing that can bring on that kind of behavior. Just mind yourself. And if she's Persian… well, she had better *not* be Persian. That's all."

Josh glanced over at Firuzeh. She looked back at him and shrugged.

Josh returned to the computer screen. He dwelt on it for a moment longer, then his mind floated off elsewhere. There was one thing he was waiting for, and that was the moment when the spreadsheet was complete, and he could clock out of work.

***

That evening, he cycled down to Santa Monica.

He had arranged to meet Sepideh on the pier. She was standing at the entrance when he arrived. She was leaned against the railing, reading a book, wind disrupting her hair a little, her thin body golden against a blue dress. She was wearing large sunglasses, which hid her eyes.

When she saw him, she folded over the top corner of the page and raised her sunglasses onto the top of her head. He took her in his arms. There was a moment of hesitation–uncertainty whether they would resume where they left off last time–then he kissed her on the lips, and there was a mutual sensation of melting. They separated. He stood back with his hands on her shoulders.

"Good day?" she said.

"Not bad. I spent most of it thinking about you." He looked at her book. "What are you reading?"

"Something about interior design. Come on," she said. "Let's go."

They took each other's hands and started to walk down the wooden ramp from the road to the pier. Taxis drove beside them, clattering as they passed over the slatted planks of wood. They passed couples and families, children excitedly skipping ahead, enticed by the rides further down the pier. Their chatter filled the air, like swallows chirruping at dusk.

At the bottom of the ramp, they passed onto the beach. Josh walked with Sepideh in one hand and his bike in the other, the wheels rolling unsteadily over the bumpy sand.

"It's easier without shoes," she said. They stopped to take them off, then continued, swinging them by their sides.

"I always prefer this side of the beach," she said.

"Which side?"

"This side. To the north of the pier. It's quieter. The south is too busy. But up here you can find space to yourself. Space to think."

They continued walking, feet stumbling over the uneven sand. They passed the beach-front houses, painted bright pastel colors, and the steep, dark cliffs that fell down from Santa Monica.

They began to leave everything behind. Soon, there were just rocks and cliffs to their right. The sounds of the pier were inaudible. The beach was empty, just an expanse of foot-churned sand and, away in the distance, a solitary blue hut on stilts, an orange float hanging outside.

"Sit down?" Josh said, stopping in his tracks.

They dropped their shoes and sat down cross-legged. The water was blue and still, the gentle waves barely breaking on the beach. The evening light cast an occasional golden shimmer on the surface. They sat looking out across the ocean.

"You know," Josh said, "when I first came to California, I never actually thought it would be like this."

"Like what?"

"I never realized there were actually little blue huts with orange floats hanging outside."

"Oh…"

"I thought it was just part of *Baywatch*. I couldn't believe it when it was actually real."

"You were a big fan?"

"Devoted. Some families went to church on Sunday morning. We watched *Baywatch* on Saturday afternoon. You?"

"Couldn't get it in Iran. Banned. Just a bit too much flesh on display."

They fell silent, the sound of waves lapping at the shore and distant traffic from Santa Monica above them.

"So," she said, "seeing as you're such a fan, why don't you show me your best *Baywatch* impression?"

"What do you mean?"

"You know… do what they do in the show. When there's a *crisis*. Sprint across the beach like you're about to save someone from a jellyfish or something."

"I don't recall that episode."

"I'm pretty sure it happened."

"It's OK, I'll give that one a miss."

"Come on…"

"Why…?"

"Because it'll be funny. I want to see you do it."

"I'll make a fool out of myself."

"It's only me watching…"

"It'll be awful…"

"Oh, go on…"

He paused, re-thinking.

"If I do it, you have to promise not to look."

"I promise."

"And you owe me a favor in return."

"Well, maybe…"

He got up slowly and dusted off the sand. "You've only asked me because you want to see me naked."

"God forbid. Underwear stays on, please."

Pulling off his T-shirt, he regretted all the wasted opportunities to go to the gym since moving to LA. Then he got his trousers stuck while trying to pull them off, hobbling around on the sand like he'd been stung on the foot by a wasp.

"Right," he said finally. "David Hasselhoff, watch and weep."

There didn't seem to be anyone in the hut, so he walked a few steps up the ramp. Then he stood leaning over the side, looking out across the beach, like a king surveying his territory.

He heard a shriek from Sepideh and saw her pointing out to sea.

He started off down the ramp at a brisk pace, like someone walking to the office. Then he broke into a trot, then finally a wild, ungainly sprint. When he arrived at the water, his legs gave way and sent him sprawling into the ocean, arms flapping about. He rolled around in the shallows for a few moments, pretending to wrestle something. Then, finally, he triumphed, shook himself down, and traipsed back up the beach. Sepideh had gotten up and was standing closer to the shore. She gave him a slow clap as he returned.

"Sensational. Academy award nomination."

He bowed gracefully. "I've been perfecting that routine for a while now."

"That jellyfish put up quite a fight..."

"It was a near-run thing. But there was only ever going to be one winner. OK," he said, shaking the water out of his ears, "your turn now."

"No way," she said, a steely look in her face.

"Spoil sport..."

"Not if you pay me."

"Come on..."

"No way... absolutely not... anything but..."

"I did it."

"That was your choice."

"OK, OK," he said eventually. "I'll leave it..." He looked away. "... but it can't stop me doing this!"

He turned around and, in one deft movement, knelt down beside Sepideh, slid his arms under her body, and scooped her up off the sand.

"Josh, don't you dare."

"I did it for you..."

She flailed her arms but he was already carrying her briskly towards the sea.

"You better not. You *absolutely* better not…"

"I gave you your chance…"

"Josh, if you get even an inch of me wet…"

"We're at the beach… we're meant to get wet…"

When they reached the water, she put up a last ditch effort, clinging onto him so he couldn't lower her in. But she couldn't stop him and, after a brief struggle, they both collapsed, a messy heap landing together in the shallows with a splash.

"This is unforgivable, Josh," she said, gasping for breath. "This is the last time you will ever see me."

He splashed water at her. "You started it!"

"You've ruined my dress."

"I'll buy you a new one…"

They splashed around for a bit, Sepideh too dazed to muster the energy to get out. Finally, she hauled herself to the shore, and Josh followed. They walked back up the beach to where he had left his clothes. Josh stopped and looked out across the water.

"There's something about the ocean," he said.

"What?"

"I don't know. Something about the way it opens up your mind. Sure, it's there, physically, right in front of you. But it also does something to your head. Breathes air into it."

Sepideh smiled. "You're getting all poetic."

"I guess you must have brought it on."

Pause.

"What does the ocean make you think about?" he said.

"Not sure," she said. "Never thought about it. I guess… the passing of time. And the future. Seeing friends growing up, seeing them move on. The dull drumbeat of life, steadily marching on."

"OK, who's the poetic one now?"

They stood, looking out towards the ocean. Then he turned to face her. She remained staring ahead. He leaned forward, tilted his head, brought his mouth up slowly to her ear, and paused for a moment. He kissed it gently.

She wormed her neck away to shrug off the sensation.

"That tickles."

He stopped. She moved her head back to where it had been
before. They stood together for a few moments, her looking out
to sea, him looking at her profile. He leaned forward again,
pausing just beside her face, then tilted his head and kissed her
neck. This time she didn't shrink away. She moved her head so
that it rested against his.

Then she turned to face him.

"You must stop tickling me," she said.

"I'm sorry."

They stood, heads held in position against each other. Then, in
mutual longing, they reached for each other. She put her hand on
his shoulder, he took the back of her head. And, as a wind came
in from the ocean, they kissed and each felt their body floating
off in the breeze.

Chapter 24

The next few weeks were idyllic. Sepideh and Josh spent their evenings together, down on Venice beach, at her gallery, at events around town. Their lives played out a succession of clichés–a montage sequence from a romantic comedy: spooning food into each other's mouths in restaurants, Sepideh clinging onto him during a horror movie at the cinema, chasing each other on the beach, walking hand in hand along the seashore.

By now, it was the middle of May. Summer was brewing, the temperature rising, the city slowly beginning to bake in the heat. An occasional light breeze made the palm trees sway against the deep-blue sky. But mainly it was just relentless, beating sunshine.

Life at *Telikani-Rezvani* ground to a standstill. Even in the air-conditioned offices of LA's glass tower blocks, the heat seemed to sap the life out of people. Employees sat around listlessly, slumped in chairs, gazing beyond their computer screens to the city beyond.

"Josh," Firuzeh said one day, "you need to cool down. Have some ice cream." She offered him two tubs. "What flavor would you like? Saffron rosewater, or ginger and lavender?"

"Thanks, Firuzeh. I'll have ginger and lavender."

"Don't forget," said Fred, appearing at the door. "Persians invented ice cream…"

"Morning Fred," Firuzeh said. "How are you?"

"All the better for this piece of news." He held up a newspaper clipping he was carrying.

"What's that?"

"You remember that piece of land? The one I saw an advert for in the paper?"

"In Tehran?"

"Just outside. Damavand."

"Well?" Firuzeh said.

"It's a notice to come and reclaim it. From last week's *Tehran Times*. I have three months. Then the government take it for good."

"So, you'll go?"

"Yes. I mean, probably. I want to." He smiled. "At least if I go back, I'll have respect. People will listen to me."

"Well, go."

"But there's the business. And the family…"

"But you've always wanted to go back."

"I know. And I promised I'd spend my old age with cousin Behzad, back on the farm."

"I think you should do it Fred…"

He fell silent and thought for a moment. "We'll see," he said.

***

That evening, Josh and Sepideh were in her apartment down in Venice. Josh was lazing on the couch reading a magazine while Sepideh worked at her computer, designing her gallery website. Through the white airy room breathed a cool ocean breeze.

"Hun," Sepideh said, stopping typing and turning to him. "You know I've got this exhibition coming up… I need an idea for a name."

"What's it about?"

"Second-generation Iranian artists. So, I was thinking, second-gen… second-gen… something…"

"How about… Sepideh's sizzling… sexy … second gen–"

"That's silly," she said, throwing her pen at him. Clutching his arm, he got up and dragged himself along the floor to the table.

"Quick… rush me to the emergency room…"

She frowned her look of mock disapproval and closed her computer. "Come on," she said. "We can't sit around here all day. We're starting to become permanently vegetative. We might sprout roots down into the floor soon, and then we'll never leave the apartment again."

"But lazing around is wonderful," Josh said, still lying on the floor.

"No, come on. We need to go out. What can we do?"

"How about a walk around Venice?"

"We always do that."

"Well, what then?"

"Let's go to West Hollywood," she said. "I know a nice little place there."

"Persian food?"

"No. You know I don't like Persian food in LA. It's always the same. Chelo kebab, chelo kebab, chelo kebab. As if there's no other Iranian food."

"Burgers," Josh blurted out. "I feel like a burger."

"You know, we really ought to be eating more *vegetarian* food," she said.

"The odd burger once in a while never hurt anyone."

"Hun… what about the future of the planet?"

"You always get to choose."

"I don't think that's true."

"Let me pick something for once…"

"I thought you chose last week?"

She turned her head away, looking at him with the side of her face–a habit she had developed recently to show she was unimpressed.

"OK," he said, sighing. "You always cause me such headaches." He noticed her smile. "But you do make me laugh."

"That's what girlfriends are for," she said. "Headaches and laughs." She kissed him on the forehead while he lay on the floor. "Come on. Let's go."

They got their stuff together and moved into their going out routine. Josh got his coat. Sepideh stood at the mirror applying makeup. She finished with the lipstick, puckered her lips together, and popped the lid back on the tube.

As usual, Sepideh drove. She didn't quite trust Josh with her car yet, and she found his driving slow. That night, the freeway was empty and they coasted easily along the fast lane.

"Stop grimacing like that, Josh."

"Like what?"

"Like I'm driving too fast. You know how I drive. Just get used to it."

They passed the rest of the journey in silence.

In West Hollywood, they found street parking then walked around the corner to the diner. Through the glass doors, they passed the black and white checked counter top, and rows of gleaming soda fountains. They slid into one of the booths with pink leather seats. The menus were large pieces of laminated card. They sat reading until the waiter arrived.

"You order," Josh said.

"No, you go."

"But you always get annoyed…"

"I don't get annoyed…"

"OK, OK, I'll go. I'll get…" he scanned the menu, "a rosewater chicken burger."

"And to drink?" asked the waiter.

"Orange blossom cola."

"Very good. And for you, madam?"

"I'll have a quarter-pounder veggie burger… with pomegranate molasses. And an orange blossom cola, too."

"Very good," he said, efficiently sliding the menu cards out of their hands.

The drinks arrived swiftly. They sat sipping at them through straws.

"Josh…" Sepideh said after a while.

"This sounds ominous…"

She scowled. "Why should it be ominous?"

"Something in your tone of voice."

"It's nothing much. All I wanted to ask was… who have you told about me?"

"Told about you?"

"Yes. I mean, who knows about me. In your life."

"Oh, right. Lots of people."

"Who?"

"Well, I issued a formal notice to my extended family. I alerted my college alumni group… my utility company…"

"Be sensible."

"Sorry. Just my immediate family. My parents. My sister. Why?"

"No reason."

He took a sip of his cola. "Who have you told about me?"

"No one…"

"I know I'm silly, but I hope I'm not that embarrassing."

"It's not that. It's just…"

"I'd bring dishonor upon your family?"

"No. It's just… I can't. It's…" she put down her drink. "People are super-gossipy. I'd prefer it if people didn't know about us."

Josh felt a slight jab of pain. "That's OK," he said, trying to shrug it off.

"It's just, if people know that I'm dating someone… well, I'd just prefer it if they didn't."

"Because it's a scandal?"

"No. Just… things are like that. In the Persian community."

"Right. Because what… you have to be a virgin when you get married?"

"Well, kind of… it's an issue, Josh. I might have to get myself sewn up."

"I'm sorry?"

"You know… sewn back up. Re-virginized."

"You mean… literally?"

"Some women get themselves sewn back up before their wedding night. Their husbands expect a virgin. So they need to be a virgin."

"Are you serious…?"

"And if it'll save me some stress and complications…"

"Wow…"

She broke into a smile again. "No, don't be ridiculous. Not me. I've just heard of people doing it, that's all."

The waiter arrived with their burgers, slid the plates onto the table, then disappeared. They each filled them with condiments: Sepideh with mayo, Josh with ketchup.

"Anyway," she said, putting the top of the burger bun back, "the point is, I just don't feel ready for people to know about us. I will. But just not now." She lifted her burger and took a bite.

They ate in silence for several minutes, looking around the diner occasionally for a source of distraction, but finding none. Sometimes these moments were uncomfortable. It felt like they had turned into one of those couples who go out for dinner on a Saturday night and just sit in silence, not saying anything to each other.

After a while, Sepideh leaned across to the pot of fresh herbs on the table, picked off some leaves, and began tearing them into shreds.

"What are you doing?" Josh said, pausing from eating his burger.

"What do you mean?"

"You're eating raw herbs."

"What's wrong with that?"

"Nothing."

She dabbed at her mouth with a napkin, then put it down. "You think it's weird."

"No."

"Yes, you do."

She pushed the pot of herbs aside, and sat looking at Josh with a puzzled expression.

"Sometimes I wonder about us, Josh."

"Why?"

"We're kind of… different."

"Look, it's a free world. If you want to eat raw herbs, that's fine. I'm not the Gestapo–"

"It's not about the herbs…"

"Well…"

"It's just… little things. Sometimes you don't get me."

"I don't understand."

"Like…" she thought for a moment. "… like when you came over that time, when we first got together. And I put orange peel in the rice."

"Yeah…?"

"You found that weird."

"Not in a bad way."

"OK… but you still found it weird. Or when we ran into my friends the other day, and it took us forever to say hello."

"That was a bit strange. How many times do you have to ask how someone's family are?"

"Well, that's just how we do things."

Josh couldn't think of anything to say. He just took a bite of his burger and sat there, chewing silently.

"You know," she said, "part of the reason I haven't introduced you to my family is that I'm worried what would happen."

"How do you mean?"

"How they would react. How *you* would react."

"I'm not some kind of social incompetent. I know how to interact with people."

"But, if you find me eating raw herbs weird, well, I sort of dread what might happen if you met my family."

"What, they *only* eat raw herbs? Or... they're vampires? They'll eat me alive?"

"Oh, they're capable of far worse."

"I see."

"No... like, I might bring you home and they might *deliberately* only speak Persian just to make you feel left out."

"I'm sure they wouldn't."

"... and even if they didn't do that, they'd probably drag you around to family occasions four or five nights of the week until you collapse."

"I could handle that."

"You say that, and other people say that, but the fact is some people *can't* handle it. And they run away."

There was a pause. They fell into silence and looked at each other.

"I know someone whose Dad offered her $50,000 not to marry some American guy. They just couldn't face it. He told her that she was Persian, and her boyfriend is what they call a non-Persian."

"Well, look," Josh said. "If you think the gap between us is really that big..."

"No, no," she said. Then she sighed, placed her elbows on the table, and sank her chin into her hands. There was a long silence.

"Josh, the thing is... if I'm in a relationship, I want it to feel right..."

"That's OK..."

"I don't want to feel uncertain..."

"Fair enough..."

"And, looking ahead, I don't... I don't want to become *torshideh.*"

"I'm sorry?"

"*Torshideh*. It means sour. Like a sour cherry."

"Right."

"You know, I don't want to become… past my prime." She fell silent. "A cherry can be the finest, ripest fruit, but once you're *torshideh*…"

They sat quietly. The waiter appeared and started clearing their plates.

"What are you thinking?" she said, once he had gone.

"About cherries. You've made me think I should have got dessert."

"Tch," she said, rolling her eyes. "You never listen. Come on," she said, getting up. "Let's go."

They paid the check at the counter on the way out. As they stepped out onto Santa Monica Boulevard, they felt the warmth of the nighttime air around them. They walked along the sidewalk, past the West Hollywood bars that were starting to fill up. In the street, yellow taxis had started prowling for fares.

They turned up the side street where they had parked. At the car, Sepideh walked round to the driver's side and Josh stood by the passenger door. She unlocked the car, and was just about to get in, when she stopped. She looked at Josh across the roof.

"Josh?"

"Yes?" he said, holding the door open.

"Can I ask you one other thing?"

"Sure."

"It's just a small thing that's been bugging me."

"Go ahead."

"I wondered…" She paused, looked away down the street, then back at him. "Just out of curiosity, since you came to LA, how many other girls have you dated?"

He shrugged. "Not many."

"How many?"

"I don't know… not many."

"Come on, you're not bad looking." She looked at him across the roof. "You must have done OK for yourself."

"I don't really keep count of these things."

There was a pause. He felt uncomfortable, standing there. He wanted to get in the car but he felt the conversation wasn't quite over.

"Why do you ask?"

"No reason."

"No, come on…"

"Well… I wondered what kind of a guy you are."

"What do you mean?"

"Are you a 'one woman for life' kind of guy, or a 'let's play the field' kind of guy?"

"Oh, OK. Now I see where this is heading."

"It's not heading anywhere. I was just curious."

They fell silent. Josh looked away down the street, then back at Sepideh.

"What about you?" he said.

"What about me?"

"How many guys have you been with?"

She scowled, showing him the side of her face. "That's not for you to know."

"Come on. How many?"

"Not many."

"But, some, at least?"

"Well, probably not as many as there should have been."

"What do you mean?"

"I don't know. I'm not sure what I've been doing with myself."

"But you're not… unattractive."

"Oh, thanks." She sighed. "Yeah, I don't know why. Working too hard, perhaps."

They paused again and stood looking over the car roof at each other. Then she looked into his eyes more firmly.

"Josh, there's something else I wanted to say."

"Go on."

"I'm fond of you…"

He remained silent, waiting for her to continue.

"But, if, for any reason…"

"Any reason, what?"

"If, for any reason, you think you don't feel the same way about me as I do about you, then…" her sentence fizzled out.

167

"I understand," he said after a moment.

"Just… I'd want to know. That's all."

"Sepideh," Josh said, holding her gaze firmly. "I… look, let's not talk about this, OK?"

She looked at him a moment longer. Josh held her gaze. Then, she ducked her head, and got into the car. Josh remained where he was, looking out across the street, then followed her inside.

Chapter 25

A week later, Josh was sitting in the garden at home. Since the arrival of summer, the garden had turned into a retreat, a paradise away from the heat. With water dappling and gushing, birds zipping in and out, and insects sheltering from the sun, it was like a sanctuary in the middle of a desert.

Nima was out, feeding the birds again. Josh remembered how he had been doing this when he first arrived. Nearly a whole year had passed.

"More food for the humming birds?"

Nima nodded.

Josh had noticed another change in Nima recently. The shiny suits had disappeared. He seemed to have reverted back to his previous appearance: baggy hippie trousers, open-toed sandals, and the goatee beard was re-growing.

"What happened to the political scheme, Nima?"

"Oh," he said, absorbed in his task, "it didn't come to anything."

"How come?"

"I guess I wasn't suited to politics."

There was a silence. Nima continued to spoon food into the wooden box. Josh sat in the hammock.

"So, what are you doing now?"

"Now, I am tending my garden. Devoting my energy to nature. Something that will always be there for me and will always appreciate me."

He withdrew the spoon from the humming bird box and turned to face Josh.

"I will just sit here, tend my garden and gaze out towards the Pacific Ocean. And think about how the waters that wash up on these shores may have touched the hands of people back in the Persian Gulf."

He put the spoon back in the jar of nectar and closed the hatch on the box.

"Anyway," he said, "what about you? How are things with your new lady?"

"Oh, yeah, they're OK."

"It must be getting pretty serious by now."

"Kind of…"

"How long has it been?"

"About three months."

"You're getting to the critical moment…"

"I guess…"

"So, where do you think things are heading?"

"I'm not sure. Haven't really thought about it."

"Wedding bells in the air?"

"I don't know about that."

"Will we hear the patter of tiny feet?"

"Early days for that, I think…"

They fell into silence. All of a sudden, there was a sharp sound from upstairs: the bleeping of Josh's phone, shrill and piercing through the air.

Josh let it continue for a bit, hoping it would eventually ring off, but it kept going.

"OK," he said, easing himself out of the hammock. "I'm coming."

He walked through the garden to the house, passing through the front door. The phone was still ringing. He quickened his pace. He sped up as he went up the stairs. Usually people rang off. This time, it just kept ringing.

At last, he burst through into his room. The phone was lying on his desk, the screen flashing on and off like the warning lamp of a lighthouse.

He didn't recognize the number. He paused for a moment, wondering whether to bother answering, but the persistence of the caller made him curious. He hit the green button and put the phone to his ear.

"Hello?"

There was a brief pause down the line, then he heard a female voice.

"Hello. Is that Josh?"

"Yes." The voice sounded familiar but he couldn't place it. "Who's this?"

"You don't remember?"

It did sound familiar, but he couldn't quite pin it down.

"No, I... I don't recognize it."

"It's your old friend..."

"Old friend...?"

"Your old friend from college..."

"From college... right, let me see..."

"It's Yasmin."

There was a pause. Josh felt his breath leave him for a moment.

"You still there?"

"Yes," he said. "I'm here."

"I know we've been out of touch for ages," she said. "But I thought you'd at least remember my voice."

"I'm sorry," he said. "You just... took me by surprise."

Another pause.

"How are you?" she said.

"I'm fine. And you?"

"Good, thanks. Just got back from traveling."

"Yeah? How was it?"

"Good, in the end. But it turned out a year on the road was long enough. What about you–where are you? What are you up to?"

"I'm in LA."

"Oh, wow. So, that plan came off? How's it been treating you?"

"Yeah, not bad."

"You managed to adjust? I wasn't sure how long you'd cope."

"It was difficult at first, but I survived. So," he said, "where are you?"

"I'm in LA, too. Just got back last week."

"Right."

"Yeah."

There was another pause.

"So," she said, "perhaps... we should meet up?"

"Well..."

"It'd be nice to see you..."

"Yeah, I guess that would be nice..."

"It's been a long time. It'd be good to hear your news."

"Sure. Be nice to hear yours, too."

"So," she said, "you around this week?"

"This week… let me see…"

"Or, we can try another time. It's not urgent."

"No, no…" Josh replied. "I can manage this week."

"When would be good?"

"How about… Sunday?"

"Yes, that could work," Yasmin said.

"Afternoon? Around three?"

"Sure."

"OK," Josh said. "I'll be down in Westwood, so perhaps somewhere on the coast. Santa Monica?"

"All right…"

"We could meet at the intersection of Broadway and Third Street Promenade at three. There's a milkshake store. See you out the front of that."

"Great," she said. "Sounds good."

There was another pause.

"It'll be good to see you," she said.

"Yes. Be good to see you, too."

"OK, well, I'll see you Sunday."

"Yes," he said. "See you then."

She hung up.

Josh pressed the red button on his phone and put it down on the desk. He looked at it for a moment, as if he didn't quite trust it, as if he didn't quite believe he'd just had that conversation.

He remained standing for a few minutes. He felt dazed. Slightly stunned. The room seemed to go hazy, like a blurry photograph. Then, as the blood returned to his brain, things came back into focus. Clarity returned. He looked around the room. Things seemed normal. He didn't feel faint any more.

He looked out the window. The garden was a multitude of shades of green. Beyond the garden, through the trees, he could just make out the ocean. And, far in the distance, he saw the hazy line of the Pacific, the sun reflected in the water, the golden light rippling on its surface.

Chapter 26

For the next two days, Josh's head turned over question after question, like his brain itself was doing somersaults.

On the Sunday, he cycled down to Santa Monica. He locked up his bike and began walking along Broadway. He felt the heat of the late afternoon sun and the steady warm glow from the asphalt. He reached the intersection of Broadway and Third Street Promenade, waiting for the lights to turn.

Then he saw her. She was standing at the street corner on the opposite side. For a moment, he wasn't sure what to do. They silently acknowledged each other with a smile and a wave. When the lights went green, for a moment they couldn't decide who should cross and who should stay. Finally, Josh made his way over. On the other side, they kissed on the cheek.

"I thought we were both going to cross there," he said.

"We'd have ended up in the middle of the road. Flattened like pancakes."

He stood back to look at her. She was just as he remembered her. The freckles on the top of her nose, the wispy black streaks of hair on her cheeks, no glitter now, just a tinge of red. She wore big sunglasses that made her look like an insect. She raised them onto the top of her head.

"Hey, you got a sun tan," she said.

"I had to. I felt really pale when I arrived."

"And you've been working out."

"Yeah, OK, you can cut the sarcasm. I'm still a stick insect."

He noticed a faded butterfly on her ankle. "I see you've got the obligatory traveler's tattoo. Not at all clichéd."

"They're cool, OK? I know the whole world's got them. But they're still cool."

Pause. Slight awkwardness. The initial cheerfulness wore off for a moment and self-consciousness seemed to be creeping in.

"So..." she said, "what do you want to do?"

"Well, we could just walk."

"Fine by me."

They set off up Third Street Promenade. Along the sidewalk

milled the usual assortment of people: tourists, couples strolling hand in hand, children dragging their parents towards ice-cream parlors. They made their way past people buying souvenir hats, and twenty-somethings in yellow T-shirts with clipboards raising money for charity. They walked slowly, threading their way through the crowds.

"So," she said. "Give me some news. Has California been the *Coast of Dreams* for you?"

"Not at first. It was tough. I didn't know anyone… wasn't sure what I was doing. I got into a few sticky situations."

"That happens here…"

"But things improved after that."

"So, it's an East Coast-West Coast romance? You've fallen for the LA lifestyle?"

"Not quite. But it's not as bad as I thought it would be. Actually, I've come to enjoy some things."

"Like?"

"Like people actually using skateboards as a method of transportation. Or people breaking into spontaneous hip-hop battles in the middle of the street…"

She laughed. "Good. Glad we could be of service."

There was a brief pause. They stopped walking, turned to face each other and just stood for a moment.

"How about you?" he said. "How was traveling?"

"I guess what they say is true… travel broadens the mind and loosens the bowels. On balance, more of the former than the latter… I think."

"What did you do exactly?"

"Well, it was meant to be adventurous," she said as they resumed walking. "But, in the end, I think it was fairly conventional. I worked in France for a bit, being a nanny for children of *very* rich Europeans. Then headed through the Middle East. Spent some time on a Kibbutz. Then into India. Managed to fight the urge to join an ashram and did a really cool ecological project. However, developed dysentery. So headed to Thailand. Wheels briefly came off… I went a bit wild, full moon parties… took too many drugs and went on a mad trip… woke up a few days later in jail and had to be bailed out by my parents…”

“You serious?”

“Of course not. I was too afraid to even try the local whiskey after seeing the effect on its victims. Enough wandering naked Swedes claiming to have seen themselves in the moon put me off that.”

Josh chuckled.

“So, after that, we went into Vietnam, briefly visited China, saw the new cities springing up like forests…”

“So a totally stereotypical year of travel,” Josh said. “A westerner going wild and enjoying the world as a pleasure-ground of consumption with absolutely no contribution to the local community.”

“Oi,” Yasmin said, jabbing him in the ribs. “I heard that.”

“And you didn’t make it to Iran?”

“If only. I thought about it. When I was in the Middle East, I could feel its pull. It was like returning home…”

“I guess you’ve come back to your real home now…”

“Sometimes I wonder what my real home is.” They stopped again, looking aimlessly into a shop window of beachwear and skateboards. “But yes, you’re right, I guess this is my real home. There comes a time when you have enough of being on the road. After a while, you need to feel like you’re not on a treadmill.”

They fell into silence and walked on a couple of minutes before either of them said anything.

“So, anyway,” she said. “I’m doing all the talking. What about you?”

“What about me?”

“You’ve got a suntan. You’ve been working out. You’ve clearly embraced the LA lifestyle.”

“Well, when in Rome…”

“And what about romance? Any flutters of the heart?”

“Oh, well… you know…”

“You know…?”

“Just… you know… the usual…”

“The usual?”

“Just… nothing special.”

“You didn’t fall for some wealthy Californian heiress, then?

That's what East-coasters usually dream of."

"Well, I may have fallen for some Californian heiresses, but I'm not sure any of them fell for *me*."

They continued walking and fell into silence again.

"Anyway," he said, "what about you? How's your boyfriend?"

"Oh, he…" her sentence fizzled out and she looked at the floor.

"What?"

"It didn't work out."

"I'm sorry to hear that."

"We split up."

There was a brief silence as they threaded their way past a group of tourists taking photos, posing with smoothies.

"Somewhere south of Bangkok. Things were OK, at first. India put a bit of a strain on things. He was totally unsympathetic while I was ill, then I returned the favor. Then, in Thailand, he made out with a lady boy."

"Quite a lot of people end up doing that…"

"Maybe, but he genuinely thought it was a woman."

"Right."

"So, anyway, that straw broke the camel's back."

"And you separated?"

"In Vietnam, he wanted to go surfing and indulge in 'Nam memorabilia. I wanted something a little more fulfilling."

"And that was it?"

"Yes. We didn't see each other again after that. For all I know, he's joined some hippie commune and is lost in the middle of the jungle."

She stopped. "Sorry," she said. "I'm probably still a bit bitter. I think we just went through some difficult times. They would have tested any relationship."

They fell into silence again as they carried on walking. They passed a group of boys break dancing; a stereo blasted while they contorted themselves into insect-like positions on a mat on the floor. A group of people had stopped to watch. Josh and Yasmin joined them for a few moments, until the audience applauded, then they resumed walking.

"So," she said, "how much longer do you plan to be here?"

"Not sure. I just recently got a job."

"Oh. Doing what?"

"Real estate."

"Real estate? Not what I pictured you doing exactly."

"I know, but it was a job, and I was desperate. Anyway, I probably won't stay for long. I've got far too familiar with all the funky things you can do in Excel. Time to move onto something else."

"Sounds sensible."

"But still in LA. No plans to leave just yet. What about you?"

"What are my plans?"

"Yes."

"I don't know really. Nothing definite. Touching base with all the family again. There's a bit of catching up to do there. But beyond that... not sure. I guess I ought to find a job."

"But you're going to stay in LA?"

"I think so. I know there are other places to see around the world, and I'm young, and should be spreading my wings, but part of me just wants to return to home base for a bit."

They stopped. They had reached the end of the promenade, where Third Street meets Wilshire Boulevard. Ahead of them lay the residential streets of Santa Monica, the rows of white apartment blocks leading up towards the hills.

They turned to face each other.

"Well," she said. "Looks like we reached the end of the road." She smiled. "It was nice to see you."

"Nice to see you, too."

"We should meet up again."

"Yes. Definitely. We should."

"You've got my number. Just give me a call sometime."

"I'll do that."

"And I'm sure you've explored lots of LA already, but if you ever want to be introduced to some hidden secrets, I'd be happy to show you around. They might be things you've seen already, but I can try."

"That would be lovely."

They smiled at each other.

"Well, I better be going now. Mom's got a lunch prepared for some distant relatives. A bunch of aunties I've never even heard of want to welcome me back home. I've got to go and smile politely for a few hours."

"OK, I better let you go."

"Give me a call though, all right?"

"Will do."

They stood on the sidewalk and looked at each other. Her eyes, which before had seemed foreign, now looked familiar, almost homely. There was silence between them, but a comfortable one.

"See you around," she said. She smiled, then raised one hand to wave, turned, and began to walk up Wilshire Boulevard.

Josh stood and watched her leave. He looked back down the Promenade. Then he looked out west, towards the beach and ocean. Through the palm trees, the water glistened, the light shimmering and sparkling off its surface. The sun was high in the sky and, for a moment, he felt blinded by the light, as if he were in the middle of an explosion. Then he turned, and began walking back down the street.

Chapter 27

The following morning, rain had swept in from the Pacific, enshrouding the city. The usual stark clarity of the sunlight was replaced by a hazy mist, the buildings looming mysteriously in the gloom. Josh spent the day sitting in the office, gazing outside at the Downtown skyscrapers. Even by his standards, it was an unproductive day. The computer screen just seemed to send him into a state of mental paralysis.

"Josh," Firuzeh said finally. "What's wrong?"

He sat there silent, glum.

"You've been staring at your screen like a zombie all day."

"Just feel a bit uninspired by spreadsheets today."

"Here, have something to eat," she said, offering him her usual bag of dried fruit and nuts.

"Thanks, Firuzeh. I'm not really hungry."

"Eh, eat something anyway."

He took a handful and chucked them in his mouth. Sitting back in his chair, he looked out the window. The mist was beginning to clear now. He could see the buildings on the opposite side of the street appearing, and a hint of sunlight shining through from behind the clouds.

He looked at the temperate gauge. It was beginning to get warmer.

***

Over the course of the day, the mist cleared, and the temperature rose. By late-afternoon, the heat was back. The sun beat down mercilessly; the radio weather report announced 104 degrees up in the Valley and only slightly less on the Westside.

When he left the office at the end of the day, Josh's mind was blurred. After the bike ride home, he stepped straight into a cool shower. He had arranged to meet Sepideh at her place in the evening. He cycled down through Santa Monica towards Venice. The evening commute was just coming to an end and he had a clear run to the coast.

As he walked up the stairs to her apartment, he noticed the French doors were open. He saw her sitting in her lounge, reading. He entered and greeted her with a kiss to the forehead.

"Good day?" she said, putting her book down.

"Not bad. Weird weather though. I think it got to my head somehow."

He plonked himself down on the couch and picked up a magazine. He tried to read but he couldn't concentrate.

"You're very quiet," she said. "Something wrong?"

"No..."

"Not like you."

"I think it's just that feeling of sadness you get at the end of a summer day. You know what I mean?"

She resumed reading her book.

They mooched around for a further hour, both subdued, a slightly uncertain silence hanging over the evening. Sepideh had cooked some *ghormeh sabzee*–herb stew–for dinner. They ate quietly.

Afterwards, Josh retired to the couch to resume reading his magazine.

"Come on," Sepideh said finally. "We can't sit around here all evening. What's on the agenda?"

"I don't know. I feel kind of lazy tonight."

"How about we do something active?"

"What, watch a movie? Go for a walk on the beach?"

"We always do those things, Josh."

"Well, I'm open to suggestions..."

"I had an idea. Tonight, it's the full moon. I thought we could go out and see it."

"That sounds like something out of *Teenwolf*. We might grow fangs and terrorize the neighbors."

"I'm serious. If you climb the Santa Monica hills, you get great views."

He put his magazine down. "Well, if you think it'll be good, then I'm down."

"It's kind of an Iranian tradition. Come on. Let's do it."

They moved into their going out routine; Sepideh did her makeup while Josh sat on the couch, putting on his shoes.

"You know," he said, calling to her in the bathroom, "you look lovely without any makeup."

She sighed. "It's easy for guys to say that. You don't know what it's like being a woman."

"No one's going to see us when we're out..."

"Maybe..."

"... and if they do, it'll be dark..."

"... but it makes me feel better."

He finished tying his shoelaces and stood up. "Right," she said, making a final close-up check of her lipstick. "Let's go."

They locked the French doors and headed down the steps to the street. When they got to the bottom, she turned to him as she always did.

"Want to drive?"

"Sure," he said, taking the keys.

It was nearly ten now. The streets through Santa Monica were empty and moonlit. At the seafront, they turned right along Pacific Coast Highway. The palm trees stood silent in the darkness and, across the ocean, a slender streak of moonlight rippled on the surface of the water.

Driving along the coast road, they soon left the city behind. Cliffs rose up on their right and, on their left, the beach gave way to rocky boulders, waves crashing against them. The road was deserted.

"Here," Sepideh said. "Turn right."

He turned off. The road wound up into the mountains. Then they turned off again, and came to a smaller road, which wound up even more steeply.

"Stop," Sepideh finally said. "From here, we can go on foot."

They stopped and climbed out of the car. Josh felt the fresh air of the hills, cool as if from an air-conditioner. They shut the doors and locked the car. Josh turned to Sepideh. "Which way?"

"There," she said, pointing to a track that led away up the hill. It was just visible in the dark.

They set off along the path, the only sound the scrunch of gravel under their feet. At first, they walked under trees, but they soon left them behind, and the hills became barren and open. From time to time, they stopped and looked up at the night sky.

Clouds swept across steadily, passing in front of the moon, their ragged edges illuminated by its light. Then, as they were carried past, the moon shone out, its glow lighting up the hillside around them.

"Sepideh…" Josh said, as they walked.

She stopped and turned around. "Yes?"

He paused. "Nothing."

"What?"

"No, sorry. Nothing."

As they approached the summit, the hill became steeper. The path narrowed and, at times, they had to scramble. It wound through some boulders, then they emerged onto a flat, bare slab of rock, its surface smoothed over by countless feet before them.

They stopped and looked out at the view around them. To their right, the Pacific Ocean, deep-black except for one rippling strip of white light that ran from the beach to the horizon. To their left was the vast spread of the city–a shimmering expanse of orange light. They stood for a moment, silent.

"It makes you feel like you're in some other world," Sepideh said.

"What kind of other world?"

"Some world from the future. Like we've been beamed onto a different planet."

"As if the city's full of aliens…"

"Well, weirder things have happened in LA."

Pause.

"It's more that it makes me think about the future," she said.

"In what way?"

"It's like we're looking out on our future," she said. She put her cold hand in his. "It's like it's all laid out there in front of us. We're looking down on the city, and you and I are out there somewhere. Except, we're not in our twenties. We're 40. I'm still selling art. And you… I don't know what you're doing."

There was a pause. Josh felt a breath of wind against him. He looked up. A scrap of cloud passed in front of the moon, then its whole was revealed again. It was so bright he had to look away. He cast his gaze back towards the ocean.

"I know," she said. "I shouldn't have said that. I'm sorry. How to ruin a perfect moment."

There was a long pause.

"Sepideh," he said.

She didn't hear. She was still looking out into the distance.

"*Sepideh?*"

"Yes?" she said, turning to face him. Josh looked into her eyes. Even though it was dark, they shone out at him.

"You know when we were out the other evening, and we were talking about the future…"

"Yes…"

"Our future…"

"Yes…"

Pause. Silence.

"I don't know how to say this."

Further silence.

"The thing is…"

He felt her grip loosen in his hand.

"What I'm trying to say is…"

Her hand slipped out of his.

"What I want to say is… two days ago…"

She took a step back. He tried to look at her, but she faced away.

"The thing is, Sepideh… there's something I didn't tell you."

She was silent. Her hands had fallen loose by her side.

"Sepideh," he said, "I don't want to leave you… I want to stay with you…"

The words dried out. They stood in silence. There was still a breath of wind in the air and, in the distance, the very faint murmur of the ocean as it crept towards the shoreline.

She turned slowly. She raised her head and looked at him, redness in her eyes.

Still silent, they stood looking into each other's eyes. Then he reached out, put his arms around her back, pulling her towards him. She came close and he felt a tremble in her body. He pressed her against his chest, and he felt the warm wetness of her tears against his skin.

Then she pushed him away and began walking back the way they had come.

Chapter 28

A week later, Josh sat with Nima in the garden. He had the day off work. The previous week, *Telikani-Rezvani* had built their 1000th column and, in recognition of this, Fred had declared a holiday. Josh lay in a hammock enjoying the flowers–now in full bloom, a dazzling array of colors–while Nima moved around, watering the plants.

"You do a good job, Nima."

"Gardens need affection."

"Well, it's beautiful."

He stopped watering and put down the can. "I've got visions for this place," he said. "I want to grow things. White cherries, askari grapes, persimmons, royal loquats. Cumin and zafaran. Fresh mint to sell at the farmers market. It won't be a garden," he said, smiling. "It'll be a paradise."

Josh got out of the hammock, picked up his phone, and headed to a secluded part of the garden. There was something he'd been resisting doing. He hadn't quite felt able. But now he had to do it.

He picked up his phone. The dial tone sounded down the line, crisp and clear. Then the voice came.

"Hi, Josh. I wondered what happened to you."

"I've been busy. Sorry."

"No need to apologize. I've been pretty frantic myself. Never knew I had so many cousins."

"Look," he said, "would you like to meet up sometime?"

"Yes. That'd be nice."

"I know it's short notice, but are you doing anything today?"

"I've got to see my parents late morning, but after that I'm free."

"I wondered if you fancied going for a drive. Maybe out of the city. I feel the need to escape somewhere."

"Sure. We could drive south. Towards San Diego… Mexico. How about a trip to the border?"

"That would work. Have you got a car?"

"No. But I can borrow my parents'."

"If they're cool with that…"

"I might have to keep it a secret."

"I'd appreciate it. Shall we meet around noon?"

"Fine. I'll come and pick you up."

"OK. See you later."

They hung up. Josh returned to the main part of the garden, and put the phone back on the table.

"Heading south?" Nima said.

"Yes."

"Good idea." Nima put down the watering can and looked up at him. "You've got to keep moving," he said. "It's easy to be in love with where you're from. It's easy to fall in love with where you arrive. But the challenge is to resist that love, wherever it may tempt you."

Then he turned, tilted his can, and resumed watering.

***

She arrived outside the house at noon, as planned. As he came down the front steps, he saw her leaning across the roof of the car, sunglasses perched on her head.

"Your chauffeur has arrived…"

He stopped on the other side of the car. They looked at each other across the roof.

"You alright?" she said. "You look a bit ghostly."

"I'm OK. Just been a difficult few days."

"Well, we've got the car. Where do you want to go?"

"As I said, anywhere. Head south and see where it takes us?"

"Sure, let's go."

They hit the 405 south at Santa Monica. It was midday, the asphalt was wide and empty, and they could feel the steady *whump whump* sound under the tires. They curved through the southern districts of LA, leaving the palm trees behind, then through the industrial wastelands north of Orange County. And then they emerged, out in the open. Just past Long Beach, they saw a sign for the coast.

"Come on," Yasmin said. "The day's too nice not to hit the

beach for a bit."

They drove through residential streets for a few blocks, past derelict bungalows and weather-beaten motels. The road fizzled out as they approached the ocean. Finally, they skidded to a halt on the sand.

They took off their shoes and began walking across the beach, carrying them in their hands. It was empty, with just a few daytime sunbathers dotted around. They went down to the shore, the waves lapping the sand, and began walking slowly along its edge.

Josh stopped, knelt down, and dipped his hands in the water. "My housemate says he could only live by the ocean," he said.

"Why?"

"Because he can imagine that the waters have touched the hands of Iranian sailors somewhere back in the Gulf."

Yasmin smiled.

"Do you feel that?" he said.

"I don't know. Sometimes I'm just happy to look out to the horizon. I don't have to imagine what could be there."

They fell silent, looking out over the water.

"What are you thinking?" Yasmin said.

"Nothing. I'm just looking at the ocean." He paused. "It's like when you're looking out of a train window. You know, when you just look, and look, and look. The ocean's like that. You can look at it for hours and you don't get bored. You never get bored."

"Come on," she said, taking his hand. "We ought to get back. We've still got some driving to do."

They walked back up the beach, stopping at the road to brush the sand off their feet. They put their shoes back on and, at the car, turned to take one last look at the ocean. It was windy now; they felt it blowing hard on their faces and the sand swirled around their feet.

They got back in the car. The engine purred into life, and they started to drive.

As they set off, a cloud of sand whirled up behind them. They rejoined the freeway, a range of mountains opening up to their left, casting long vistas to the East. Ahead of them lay an empty stretch of asphalt, silent and waiting, dissolving into a shimmering watery mirage. The sun rode high in the sky and the mountains were a pastel blue. The wind buffeted them as they drove, gusting hard on the open road, and in the warm afternoon the land was flooded with light.

Thank you to the many, many people who made the research
and writing of this book possible.